The Law School Admission Council (LSAC) is a nonprofit corporation whose members are more than 200 law schools in the United States, Canada, and Australia. Headquartered in Newtown, PA, USA, the Council was founded in 1947 to facilitate the law school admission process. The Council has grown to provide numerous products and services to law schools and to approximately 85,000 law school applicants each year.

All law schools approved by the American Bar Association (ABA) are LSAC members. Canadian law schools recognized by a provincial or territorial law society or government agency are also members. Accredited law schools outside of the United States and Canada are eligible for membership at the discretion of the LSAC Board of Trustees; Melbourne Law School, the University of Melbourne is the first LSAC-member law school outside of North America.

The services provided by LSAC are the Law School Admission Test (LSAT); the Credential Assembly Service, which includes letters of recommendation, electronic applications, and domestic and international transcript processing for JD degrees; the LLM Credential Assembly Service; the Candidate Referral Service (CRS); the Admission Communication & Exchange System (ACES, ACES^2); research and statistical reports; websites for law schools and prelaw advisors (*LSACnet.org*), law school applicants (*LSAC.org*), and undergraduates from minority groups (*DiscoverLaw.org*); testing and admission-related consultations with legal educators worldwide; and various publications, videos, and LSAT preparation tools. LSAC does not engage in assessing an applicant's chances for admission to any law school; all admission decisions are made by individual law schools.

Table of Contents

The Law School Admission Test is a half-day standardized test required for admission to all ABA-approved law schools, most Canadian law schools, and many non-ABA-approved law schools. It consists of five 35-minute sections of multiple-choice questions. Four of the five sections contribute to the test taker's score. These sections include one reading comprehension section, one analytical reasoning section, and two logical reasoning sections. The unscored section, commonly referred to as the variable section, typically is used to pretest new test questions or to preequate new test forms. The placement of this section in the LSAT will vary. A 35-minute writing sample is administered at the end of the test. The writing sample is not scored by LSAC, but copies are sent to all law schools to which you apply. The score scale for the LSAT is 120 to 180.

The LSAT is designed to measure skills considered essential for success in law school: the reading and comprehension of complex texts with accuracy and insight; the organization and management of information and the ability to draw reasonable inferences from it; the ability to think critically; and the analysis and evaluation of the reasoning and arguments of others.

The LSAT provides a standard measure of acquired reading and verbal reasoning skills that law schools can use as one of several factors in assessing applicants.

For up-to-date information about LSAC's services, go to our website, *www.LSAC.org* or pick up a current *LSAC Information Book*.

Scoring

Your LSAT score is based on the number of questions you answer correctly (the raw score). There is no deduction for incorrect answers, and all questions count equally. In other words, there is no penalty for guessing.

■ Test Score Accuracy—Reliability and Standard Error of Measurement

Candidates perform at different levels on different occasions for reasons quite unrelated to the characteristics of a test itself. The accuracy of test scores is best described by the use of two related statistical terms: reliability and standard error of measurement.

Reliability is a measure of how consistently a test measures the skills being assessed. The higher the reliability coefficient for a test, the more certain we can be that test takers would get very similar scores if they took the test again.

LSAC reports an internal consistency measure of reliability for every test form. Reliability can vary from 0.00 to 1.00, and a test with no measurement error would have a reliability coefficient of 1.00 (never attained in practice). Reliability coefficients for past LSAT forms have ranged from .90 to .95, indicating a high degree of consistency for these tests. LSAC expects the reliability of the LSAT to continue to fall within the same range.

LSAC also reports the amount of measurement error associated with each test form, a concept known as the standard error of measurement (SEM). The SEM, which is usually about 2.6 points, indicates how close a test taker's observed score is likely to be to his or her true score. True scores are theoretical scores that would be obtained from perfectly reliable tests with no measurement error—scores never known in practice.

Score bands, or ranges of scores that contain a test taker's true score a certain percentage of the time, can be derived using the SEM. LSAT score bands are constructed by adding and subtracting the (rounded)

SEM to and from an actual LSAT score (e.g., the LSAT score, plus or minus 3 points). Scores near 120 or 180 have asymmetrical bands. Score bands constructed in this manner will contain an individual's true score approximately 68 percent of the time.

Measurement error also must be taken into account when comparing LSAT scores of two test takers. It is likely that small differences in scores are due to measurement error rather than to meaningful differences in ability. The standard error of score differences provides some guidance as to the importance of differences between two scores. The standard error of score differences is approximately 1.4 times larger than the standard error of measurement for the individual scores.

Thus, a test score should be regarded as a useful but approximate measure of a test taker's abilities as measured by the test, not as an exact determination of his or her abilities. LSAC encourages law schools to examine the range of scores within the interval that probably contains the test taker's true score (e.g., the test taker's score band) rather than solely interpret the reported score alone.

■ Adjustments for Variation in Test Difficulty

All test forms of the LSAT reported on the same score scale are designed to measure the same abilities, but one test form may be slightly easier or more difficult than another. The scores from different test forms are made comparable through a statistical procedure known as equating. As a result of equating, a given scaled score earned on different test forms reflects the same level of ability.

■ Research on the LSAT

Summaries of LSAT validity studies and other LSAT research can be found in member law school libraries.

■ **To Inquire About Test Questions**

If you find what you believe to be an error or ambiguity in a test question that affects your response to the question, contact LSAC by e-mail: *LSATTS@LSAC.org*, or write to Law School Admission Council, Test Development Group, Box 40, Newtown, PA 18940-0040.

How This PrepTest Differs From an Actual LSAT

This PrepTest is made up of the scored sections and writing sample from the actual disclosed LSAT administered in September 2009. However, it does not contain the extra, variable section that is used to pretest new test items of one of the three multiple-choice question types. The three multiple-choice question types may be in a different order in an actual LSAT than in this PrepTest. This is because the order of these question types is intentionally varied for each administration of the test.

The Question Types

The multiple-choice questions that make up most of the LSAT reflect a broad range of academic disciplines and are intended to give no advantage to candidates from a particular academic background.

The five sections of the test contain three different question types. The following material presents a general discussion of the nature of each question type and some strategies that can be used in answering them.

■ **Analytical Reasoning Questions**

Analytical reasoning items are designed to measure your ability to understand a structure of relationships and to draw logical conclusions about the structure. You are asked to make deductions from a set of statements, rules, or conditions that describe relationships among entities such as persons, places, things, or events. They simulate the kinds of detailed analyses of relationships that a law student must perform in solving legal problems. For example, a passage might describe four diplomats sitting around a table, following certain rules of protocol as to who can sit where. You must answer questions about the implications of the given information, for example, who is sitting between diplomats X and Y.

The passage used for each group of questions describes a common relationship such as the following:

- Assignment: Two parents, P and O, and their children, R and S, must go to the dentist on four consecutive days, designated 1, 2, 3, and 4;

- Ordering: X arrived before Y but after Z;

- Grouping: A manager is trying to form a project team from seven staff members—R, S, T, U, V, W, and X. Each staff member has a particular strength—writing, planning, or facilitating;

- Spatial: A certain country contains six cities and each city is connected to at least one other city by a system of roads, some of which are one-way.

Careful reading and analysis are necessary to determine the exact nature of the relationships involved. Some relationships are fixed (e.g., P and R always sit at the same table). Other relationships are variable (e.g., Q must be assigned to either table 1 or table 3). Some relationships that are not stated in the conditions are implied by and can be deduced from those that are stated. (e.g., If one condition about books on a shelf specifies that Book L is to the left of Book Y, and another specifies that Book P is to the left of Book L, then it can be deduced that Book P is to the left of Book Y.)

No formal training in logic is required to answer these questions correctly. Analytical reasoning questions are intended to be answered using knowledge, skills, and reasoning ability generally expected of college students and graduates.

Suggested Approach

Some people may prefer to answer first those questions about a passage that seem less difficult and then those that seem more difficult. In general, it is best not to start another passage before finishing one begun earlier, because much time can be lost in returning to a passage and reestablishing familiarity with its relationships. Do not assume that, because the conditions for a set of questions look long or complicated, the questions based on those conditions will necessarily be especially difficult.

Reading the passage. In reading the conditions, do not introduce unwarranted assumptions. For instance, in a set establishing relationships of height and weight among the members of a team, do not assume that a person who is taller than another person must weigh more than that person. All the information needed to answer each question is provided in the passage and the question itself.

The conditions are designed to be as clear as possible; do not interpret them as if they were intended to trick you. For example, if a question asks how many people could be eligible to serve on a committee, consider only those people named in the passage unless directed otherwise. When in doubt, read the conditions in their most obvious sense. Remember, however, that the language in the conditions is intended to be read for precise meaning. It is essential to pay particular attention to words that describe or limit relationships, such as "only," "exactly," "never," "always," "must be," "cannot be," and the like.

The result of this careful reading will be a clear picture of the structure of the relationships involved, including the kinds of relationships permitted, the participants in the relationships, and the range of actions or attributes allowed by the relationships for these participants.

Questions are independent. Each question should be considered separately from the other questions in its set; no information, except what is given in the original conditions, should be carried over from one question to another. In some cases a question will simply ask for conclusions to be drawn from the conditions as originally given. Some questions may, however, add information to the original conditions or temporarily suspend one of the original conditions for the purpose of that question only. For example, if Question 1 adds the information "if P is sitting at table 2 ...," this information should NOT be carried over to any other question in the group.

Highlighting the text; using diagrams. Many people find it useful to underline key points in the passage and in each question. In addition, it may prove very helpful to draw a diagram to assist you in finding the solution to the problem.

In preparing for the test, you may wish to experiment with different types of diagrams. For a scheduling problem, a calendar-like diagram may be helpful. For a spatial relationship problem, a simple map can be a useful device.

Even though some people find diagrams to be very helpful, other people seldom use them. And among those who do regularly use diagrams in solving these problems, there is by no means universal agreement on which kind of diagram is best for which problem or in which cases a diagram is most useful. Do not be concerned if a particular problem in the test seems to be best approached without the use of a diagram.

■ Logical Reasoning Questions

Logical reasoning questions evaluate your ability to understand, analyze, criticize, and complete a variety of arguments. The arguments are contained in short passages taken from a variety of sources, including letters to the editor, speeches, advertisements, newspaper articles and editorials, informal discussions and conversations, as well as articles in the humanities, the social sciences, and the natural sciences.

Each logical reasoning question requires you to read and comprehend a short passage, then answer one or two questions about it. The questions test a variety of abilities involved in reasoning logically and thinking critically. These include:

- recognizing the point or issue of an argument or dispute;

- detecting the assumptions involved in an argumentation or chain of reasoning;

- drawing reasonable conclusions from given evidence or premises;

- identifying and applying principles;

- identifying the method or structure of an argument or chain of reasoning;

- detecting reasoning errors and misinterpretations;

- determining how additional evidence or argumentation affects an argument or conclusion; and

- identifying explanations and recognizing resolutions of conflicting facts or arguments.

The questions do not presuppose knowledge of the terminology of formal logic. For example, you will not be expected to know the meaning of specialized terms such as "ad hominem" or "syllogism." On the other hand, you will be expected to understand and critique the reasoning contained in arguments. This requires that you possess, at a minimum, a college-level understanding of widely used concepts such as argument, premise, assumption, and conclusion.

Suggested Approach

Read each question carefully. Make sure that you understand the meaning of each part of the question. Make sure that you understand the meaning of each answer choice and the ways in which it may or may not relate to the question posed.

Do not pick a response simply because it is a true statement. Although true, it may not answer the question posed.

Answer each question on the basis of the information that is given, even if you do not agree with it. Work within the context provided by the passage. LSAT questions do not involve any tricks or hidden meanings.

■ Reading Comprehension Questions

The purpose of reading comprehension questions is to measure your ability to read, with understanding and insight, examples of lengthy and complex materials similar to those commonly encountered in law school work. The reading comprehension section of the LSAT contains four sets of reading questions, each consisting of a selection of reading material followed by five to eight questions. The reading selection in three of the four sets consists of a single reading passage of approximately 450 words in length. The other set contains two related shorter passages. Sets with two passages are a new variant of reading comprehension, called comparative reading, which were introduced into the reading comprehension section in June 2007. See "Comparative Reading" below for more information.

Reading selections for reading comprehension questions are drawn from subjects such as the humanities, the social sciences, the biological and physical sciences, and issues related to the law. Reading comprehension questions require you to read carefully and accurately, to determine the relationships among the various parts of the reading selection, and to draw reasonable inferences from the material in the selection. The questions may ask about the following characteristics of a passage or pair of passages:

- the main idea or primary purpose;

- the meaning or purpose of words or phrases used;

- information explicitly stated;

- information or ideas that can be inferred;

- the organization or structure;

- the application of information in a passage to a new context; and

- the author's attitude as it is revealed in the tone of a passage or the language used.

Suggested Approach

Since reading selections are drawn from many different disciplines and sources, you should not be discouraged if you encounter material with which you are not familiar. It is important to remember that questions are to be answered exclusively on the basis of the information provided in the selection. There is no particular knowledge that you are expected to bring to the test, and you should not make inferences based on any prior knowledge of a subject that you may have. You may, however, wish to defer working on a set of questions that seems particularly difficult or unfamiliar until after you have dealt with sets you find easier.

Strategies. In preparing for the test, you should experiment with different strategies and decide which work most effectively for you. These include:

- reading the selection very closely and then answering the questions;

- reading the questions first, reading the selection closely, and then returning to the questions; or

- skimming the selection and questions very quickly, then rereading the selection closely and answering the questions.

Remember that your strategy must be effective for you under timed conditions.

Reading the selection. Whatever strategy you choose, you should give the passage or pair of passages at least one careful reading before answering the questions. Try to distinguish main ideas from supporting ideas, and opinions or attitudes from factual, objective information. Note transitions from one idea to the next and examine the relationships among the different ideas or parts of a passage, or between the two passages in comparative reading sets. Consider how and why an author makes points and draws conclusions. Be sensitive to implications of what the passages say.

You may find it helpful to mark key parts of passages. For example, you might underline main ideas or important arguments, and you might circle transitional words—"although," "nevertheless," "correspondingly," and the like—that will help you map the structure of a passage. Moreover, you might note descriptive words that will help you identify an author's attitude toward a particular idea or person.

Answering the Questions

- Always read all the answer choices before selecting the best answer. The best answer choice is the one that most accurately and completely answers the question being posed.

- Respond to the specific question being asked. Do not pick an answer choice simply because it is a true statement. For example, picking a true statement might yield an incorrect answer to a question in which you are asked to identify an author's position on an issue, since here you are not being asked to evaluate the truth of the author's position but only to correctly identify what that position is.

- Answer the questions only on the basis of the information provided in the selection. Your own views, interpretations, or opinions, and those you have heard from others, may sometimes conflict with those expressed in a reading selection; however, you are expected to work within the context provided by the reading selection. You should not expect to agree with everything you encounter in reading comprehension passages.

■ Comparative Reading

As of the June 2007 administration, LSAC introduced a new variant of reading comprehension, called comparative reading, as one of the four sets in the LSAT reading comprehension section. In general, comparative reading questions are similar to traditional reading comprehension questions, except that comparative reading questions are based on two shorter passages instead of one longer passage. The two passages together are of roughly the same length as one reading comprehension passage, so the total amount of reading in the reading comprehension section remains essentially the same. A few of the questions that follow a comparative reading passage pair might concern only one of the two passages, but most will be about both passages and how they relate to each other.

Comparative reading questions reflect the nature of some important tasks in law school work, such as understanding arguments from multiple texts by applying skills of comparison, contrast, generalization, and synthesis to the texts. The purpose of comparative reading is to assess this important set of skills directly.

What Comparative Reading Looks Like

The two passages in a comparative reading set—labeled **"Passage A"** and **"Passage B"**—discuss the same topic or related topics. The topics fall into the same academic categories traditionally used in reading comprehension: humanities, natural sciences, social sciences, and issues related to the law. Like traditional reading comprehension passages, comparative reading passages are complex and generally involve argument. The two passages in a comparative reading pair are typically adapted from two different published sources written by two different authors. They are usually independent of each other, with neither author responding directly to the other.

As you read the pair of passages, it is helpful to try to determine what the central idea or main point of each passage is, and to determine how the passages relate to each other. The passages will relate to each other in various ways. In some cases, the authors of the passages will be in general agreement with each other, while in others their views will be directly opposed. Passage pairs may also exhibit more complex types of relationships: for example, one passage might articulate a set of principles, while the other passage applies those or similar principles to a particular situation.

Questions that are concerned with only one of the passages are essentially identical to traditional reading comprehension questions. Questions that address both passages test the same fundamental reading skills as traditional reading comprehension questions, but the skills are applied to two texts instead of one. You may be asked to identify a main purpose shared by both passages, a statement with which both authors would agree, or a similarity or dissimilarity in the structure of the arguments in the two passages. The following are additional examples of comparative reading questions:

- Which one of the following is the central topic of each passage?

- Both passages explicitly mention which one of the following?

- Which one of the following statements is most strongly supported by both passages?

- Which one of the following most accurately describes the attitude expressed by the author of passage B toward the overall argument in passage A?

- The relationship between passage A and passage B is most analogous to the relationship in which one of the following?

This is not a complete list of the sorts of questions you may be asked in a comparative reading set, but it illustrates the range of questions you may be asked.

The Writing Sample

On the day of the test, you will be asked to write one sample essay. LSAC does not score the writing sample, but copies are sent to all law schools to which you apply. According to a 2006 LSAC survey of 157 United States and Canadian law schools, almost all utilize the writing sample in evaluating some applications for admission. Frivolous responses or no responses to writing sample prompts have been used by law schools as grounds for rejection of applications for admission.

In developing and implementing the writing sample portion of the LSAT, LSAC has operated on the following premises: First, law schools and the legal profession value highly the ability to communicate effectively in writing. Second, it is important to encourage potential law students to develop effective writing skills. Third, a sample of an applicant's writing, produced under controlled conditions, is a potentially useful indication of that

person's writing ability. Fourth, the writing sample can serve as an independent check on other writing submitted by applicants as part of the admission process. Finally, writing samples may be useful for diagnostic purposes.

You will have 35 minutes in which to plan and write an essay on the topic you receive. Read the topic and the accompanying directions carefully. You will probably find it best to spend a few minutes considering the topic and organizing your thoughts before you begin writing. In your essay, be sure to develop your ideas fully, leaving time, if possible, to review what you have written. Do not write on a topic other than the one specified. Writing on a topic of your own choice is not acceptable.

No special knowledge is required or expected for this writing exercise. Law schools are interested in the reasoning, clarity, organization, language usage, and writing mechanics displayed in your essay. How well you write is more important than how much you write. Confine your essay to the blocked, lined area on the front and back of the Writing Sample Response Sheet. Only that area will be reproduced for law schools. Be sure that your writing is legible.

The writing prompt presents a decision problem. You are asked to make a choice between two positions or courses of action. Both of the choices are defensible, and you are given criteria and facts on which to base your decision. There is no "right" or "wrong" position to take on the topic, so the quality of each test taker's response is a function not of which choice is made, but of how well or poorly the choice is supported and how well or poorly the other choice is criticized.

Taking the PrepTest Under Simulated LSAT Conditions

One important way to prepare for the LSAT is to simulate the day of the test by taking a practice test under actual time constraints. Taking a practice test under timed conditions helps you to estimate the amount of time you can afford to spend on each question in a section and to determine the question types on which you may need additional practice.

Since the LSAT is a timed test, it is important to use your allotted time wisely. During the test, you may work only on the section designated by the test supervisor. You cannot devote extra time to a difficult section and make up that time on a section you find easier. In pacing yourself, and checking your answers, you should think of each section of the test as a separate minitest.

Be sure that you answer every question on the test. When you do not know the correct answer to a question, first eliminate the responses that you know are incorrect, then make your best guess among the remaining choices. Do not be afraid to guess as there is no penalty for incorrect answers.

When you take a practice test, abide by all the requirements specified in the directions and keep strictly within the specified time limits. Work without a rest period. When you take an actual test, you will have only a short break—usually 10-15 minutes—after SECTION III. When taken under conditions as much like actual testing conditions as possible, a practice test provides very useful preparation for taking the LSAT.

Official directions for the four multiple-choice sections and the writing sample are included in this PrepTest so that you can approximate actual testing conditions as you practice.

To take the test:

- Set a timer for 35 minutes. Answer all the questions in SECTION I of this PrepTest. Stop working on that section when the 35 minutes have elapsed.

- Repeat, allowing yourself 35 minutes each for sections II, III, and IV.

- Set the timer again for 35 minutes, then prepare your response to the writing sample topic at the end of this PrepTest.

- Refer to "Computing Your Score" for the PrepTest for instruction on evaluating your performance. An answer key is provided for that purpose.

The practice test that follows consists of four sections corresponding to the four scored sections of the September 2009 LSAT. Also reprinted is the September 2009 unscored writing sample topic.

General Directions for the LSAT Answer Sheet

The actual testing time for this portion of the test will be 2 hours 55 minutes. There are five sections, each with a time limit of 35 minutes. The supervisor will tell you when to begin and end each section. If you finish a section before time is called, you may check your work on that section only; do not turn to any other section of the test book and do not work on any other section either in the test book or on the answer sheet.

There are several different types of questions on the test, and each question type has its own directions. Be sure you understand the directions for each question type before attempting to answer any questions in that section.

Not everyone will finish all the questions in the time allowed. Do not hurry, but work steadily and as quickly as you can without sacrificing accuracy. You are advised to use your time effectively. If a question seems too difficult, go on to the next one and return to the difficult question after completing the section. MARK THE BEST ANSWER YOU CAN FOR EVERY QUESTION. NO DEDUCTIONS WILL BE MADE FOR WRONG ANSWERS. YOUR SCORE WILL BE BASED ONLY ON THE NUMBER OF QUESTIONS YOU ANSWER CORRECTLY.

ALL YOUR ANSWERS MUST BE MARKED ON THE ANSWER SHEET. Answer spaces for each question are lettered to correspond with the letters of the potential answers to each question in the test book. After you have decided which of the answers is correct, blacken the corresponding space on the answer sheet. BE SURE THAT EACH MARK IS BLACK AND COMPLETELY FILLS THE ANSWER SPACE. Give only one answer to each question. If you change an answer, be sure that all previous marks are erased completely. Since the answer sheet is machine scored, incomplete erasures may be interpreted as intended answers. ANSWERS RECORDED IN THE TEST BOOK WILL NOT BE SCORED.

There may be more questions noted on this answer sheet than there are questions in a section. Do not be concerned but be certain that the section and number of the question you are answering matches the answer sheet section and question number. Additional answer spaces in any answer sheet section should be left blank. Begin your next section in the number one answer space for that section.

LSAC takes various steps to ensure that answer sheets are returned from test centers in a timely manner for processing. In the unlikely event that an answer sheet(s) is not received, LSAC will permit the examinee to either retest at no additional fee or to receive a refund of his or her LSAT fee. THESE REMEDIES ARE THE EXCLUSIVE REMEDIES AVAILABLE IN THE UNLIKELY EVENT THAT AN ANSWER SHEET IS NOT RECEIVED BY LSAC.

Score Cancellation

Complete this section only if you are absolutely certain you want to cancel your score. A CANCELLATION REQUEST CANNOT BE RESCINDED. IF YOU ARE AT ALL UNCERTAIN, YOU SHOULD NOT COMPLETE THIS SECTION.

To cancel your score from this administration, you must:

A. fill in both ovals here ..... ○○
    AND

B. read the following statement. Then sign your name and enter the date.
    YOUR SIGNATURE ALONE IS NOT SUFFICIENT FOR SCORE CANCELLATION. BOTH OVALS ABOVE MUST BE FILLED IN FOR SCANNING EQUIPMENT TO RECOGNIZE YOUR REQUEST FOR SCORE CANCELLATION.

I certify that I wish to cancel my test score from this administration. I understand that my request is irreversible and that my score will not be sent to me or to the law schools to which I apply.

_____
Sign your name in full

_____
Date

HOW DID YOU PREPARE FOR THE LSAT?
(Select all that apply.)

Responses to this item are voluntary and will be used for statistical research purposes only.

○ By studying the sample questions in the LSAT & LSDAS Information Book.
○ By taking the free sample LSAT in the LSAT & LSDAS Information Book.
○ By working through official LSAT PrepTests, ItemWise, and/or other LSAC test prep products.
○ By using LSAT prep books or software not published by LSAC.
○ By attending a commercial test preparation or coaching course.
○ By attending a test preparation or coaching course offered through an undergraduate institution.
○ Self study.
○ Other preparation.
○ No preparation.

CERTIFYING STATEMENT

Please write (DO NOT PRINT) the following statement. Sign and date.

I certify that I am the examinee whose name appears on this answer sheet and that I am here to take the LSAT for the sole purpose of being considered for admission to law school. I further certify that I will neither assist nor receive assistance from any other candidate, and I agree not to copy or retain examination questions or to transmit them to or discuss them with any other person in any form.

_____
_____
_____
_____
_____
_____
_____
_____

SIGNATURE: _____ TODAY'S DATE: ___/___/___
                                                         MONTH DAY YEAR

INSTRUCTIONS FOR COMPLETING THE BIOGRAPHICAL AREA ARE ON THE BACK COVER OF YOUR TEST BOOKLET.
USE ONLY A NO. 2 OR HB PENCIL TO COMPLETE THIS ANSWER SHEET. DO NOT USE INK.

A

USE A NO. 2 OR HB PENCIL ONLY

● Right Mark   ⊘ ⊗ ⊙ Wrong Marks

1 LAST NAME   FIRST NAME   MI

2 SOCIAL SECURITY/ SOCIAL INSURANCE NO.

3 LSAC ACCOUNT NUMBER

L

4 DATE OF BIRTH

MONTH	DAY	YEAR
Jan		
Feb		
Mar		
Apr		
May		
June		
July		
Aug		
Sept		
Oct		
Nov		
Dec		

5 RACIAL/ETHNIC DESCRIPTION
Mark one or more
- 1 Aboriginal/TSI Australian
- 2 Amer. Indian/Alaska Native
- 3 Asian
- 4 Black/African American
- 5 Canadian Aboriginal
- 6 Caucasian/White
- 7 Hispanic/Latino
- 8 Native Hawaiian/Other Pacific Islander
- 9 Puerto Rican

6 GENDER
- Male
- Female

7 DOMINANT LANGUAGE
- English
- Other

8 ENGLISH FLUENCY
- Yes   - No

9 TEST BOOK SERIAL NO.

10 TEST FORM

11 TEST DATE

MONTH   DAY   YEAR

12 CENTER NUMBER

13 TEST FORM CODE

Law School Admission Test

Mark one and only one answer to each question. Be sure to fill in completely the space for your intended answer choice. If you erase, do so completely. Make no stray marks.

SECTION 1 / SECTION 2 / SECTION 3 / SECTION 4 / SECTION 5

(Each section: questions 1–30, answer choices A B C D E)

14 PLEASE PRINT ALL INFORMATION

LAST NAME   FIRST

SOCIAL SECURITY/SOCIAL INSURANCE NO.

DATE OF BIRTH

MAILING ADDRESS

NOTE: If you have a new address, you must write LSAC at Box 2000-C, Newtown, PA 18940 or call 215.968.1001.

FOR LSAC USE ONLY		
LR	LW	LCS

● Ⓑ

SECTION I
Time—35 minutes
26 Questions

<u>Directions</u>: The questions in this section are based on the reasoning contained in brief statements or passages. For some questions, more than one of the choices could conceivably answer the question. However, you are to choose the <u>best</u> answer; that is, the response that most accurately and completely answers the question. You should not make assumptions that are by commonsense standards implausible, superfluous, or incompatible with the passage. After you have chosen the best answer, blacken the corresponding space on your answer sheet.

1. Commentator: Although the present freshwater supply is adequate for today's patterns of water use, the human population will increase substantially over the next few decades, drastically increasing the need for freshwater. Hence, restrictions on water use will be necessary to meet the freshwater needs of humankind in the not-too-distant future.

    Which one of the following is an assumption required by the argument?

    (A)   Humans will adapt to restrictions on the use of water without resorting to wasteful use of other natural resources.

    (B)   The total supply of freshwater has not diminished in recent years.

    (C)   The freshwater supply will not increase sufficiently to meet the increased needs of humankind.

    (D)   No attempt to synthesize water will have an appreciable effect on the quantity of freshwater available.

    (E)   No water conservation measure previously attempted yielded an increase in the supply of freshwater available for human use.

2. Psychologist: The best way to recall a certain word or name that one is having trouble remembering is to occupy one's mind with other things, since often the more we strive to remember a certain word or name that we can't think of, the less likely it becomes that the word will come to mind.

    The principle that underlies the psychologist's argument underlies which one of the following arguments?

    (A)   Often, the best way to achieve happiness is to pursue other things besides wealth and fame, for there are wealthy and famous people who are not particularly happy, which suggests that true happiness does not consist in wealth and fame.

    (B)   The best way to succeed in writing a long document is not to think about how much is left to write but only about the current paragraph, since on many occasions thinking about what remains to be done will be so discouraging that the writer will be tempted to abandon the project.

    (C)   The best way to overcome a serious mistake is to continue on confidently as though all is well. After all, one can overcome a serious mistake by succeeding in new challenges, and dwelling on one's errors usually distracts one's mind from new challenges.

    (D)   The best way to fall asleep quickly is to engage in some mental diversion like counting sheep, because frequently the more one concentrates on falling asleep the lower the chance of falling asleep quickly.

    (E)   The best way to cope with sorrow or grief is to turn one's attention to those who are experiencing even greater hardship, for in many circumstances this will make our own troubles seem bearable by comparison.

GO ON TO THE NEXT PAGE.

3. Letter to the editor: The Planning Department budget increased from $100,000 in 2001 to $524,000 for this year. However, this does not justify your conclusion in yesterday's editorial that the department now spends five times as much money as it did in 2001 to perform the same duties.

Which one of the following, if true, most helps to support the claim made in the letter regarding the justification of the editorial's conclusion?

(A) Departments other than the Planning Department have had much larger budget increases since 2001.

(B) Since 2001, the Planning Department has dramatically reduced its spending on overtime pay.

(C) In some years between 2001 and this year, the Planning Department budget did not increase.

(D) The budget figures used in the original editorial were adjusted for inflation.

(E) A restructuring act, passed in 2003, broadened the duties of the Planning Department.

4. At mock trials in which jury instructions were given in technical legal jargon, jury verdicts tended to mirror the judge's own opinions. Jurors had become aware of the judge's nonverbal behavior: facial expressions, body movements, tone of voice. Jurors who viewed the same case but were given instruction in clear, nontechnical language, however, were comparatively more likely to return verdicts at odds with the judge's opinion.

Which one of the following is best illustrated by the example described above?

(A) Technical language tends to be more precise than nontechnical language.

(B) A person's influence is proportional to that person's perceived status.

(C) Nonverbal behavior is not an effective means of communication.

(D) Real trials are better suited for experimentation than are mock trials.

(E) The way in which a judge instructs a jury can influence the jury's verdict.

5. Doctor: While a few alternative medicines have dangerous side effects, some, such as many herbs, have been proven safe to consume. Thus, though there is little firm evidence of medicinal effect, advocates of these herbs as remedies for serious illnesses should always be allowed to prescribe them, since their patients will not be harmed, and might be helped, by the use of these products.

Which one of the following, if true, most seriously weakens the doctor's argument?

(A) Many practitioners and patients neglect more effective conventional medicines in favor of herbal remedies.

(B) Many herbal remedies are marketed with claims of proven effectiveness when in fact their effectiveness is unproven.

(C) Some patients may have allergic reactions to certain medicines that have been tolerated by other patients.

(D) The vast majority of purveyors of alternative medicines are driven as much by the profit motive as by a regard for their patients' health.

(E) Any pain relief or other benefits of many herbs have been proven to derive entirely from patients' belief in the remedy, rather than from its biochemical properties.

6. When a nation is on the brink of financial crisis, its government does not violate free-market principles if, in order to prevent economic collapse, it limits the extent to which foreign investors and lenders can withdraw their money. After all, the right to free speech does not include the right to shout "Fire!" in a crowded theatre, and the harm done as investors and lenders rush madly to get their money out before everyone else does can be just as real as the harm resulting from a stampede in a theatre.

The argument does which one of the following?

(A) tries to show that a set of principles is limited in a specific way by using an analogy to a similar principle that is limited in a similar way

(B) infers a claim by arguing that the truth of that claim would best explain observed facts

(C) presents numerous experimental results as evidence for a general principle

(D) attempts to demonstrate that an explanation of a phenomenon is flawed by showing that it fails to explain a particular instance of that phenomenon

(E) applies an empirical generalization to reach a conclusion about a particular case

GO ON TO THE NEXT PAGE.

7. Although many political candidates object to being made the target of advertising designed to cast them in an adverse light, such advertising actually benefits its targets because most elections have been won by candidates who were the targets of that kind of advertising.

The pattern of flawed reasoning in the argument most closely parallels that in which one of the following?

(A) Although many people dislike physical exercise, they should exercise because it is a good way to improve their overall health.

(B) Although many actors dislike harsh reviews of their work, such reviews actually help their careers because most of the really prestigious acting awards have gone to actors who have had performances of theirs reviewed harshly.

(C) Although many students dislike studying, it must be a good way to achieve academic success because most students who study pass their courses.

(D) Although many film critics dislike horror films, such films are bound to be successful because a large number of people are eager to attend them.

(E) Although many people dislike feeling sleepy as a result of staying up late the previous night, such sleepiness must be acceptable to those who experience it because most people who stay up late enjoy doing so.

8. Working residents of Springfield live, on average, farther from their workplaces than do working residents of Rorchester. Thus, one would expect that the demand for public transportation would be greater in Springfield than in Rorchester. However, Springfield has only half as many bus routes as Rorchester.

Each of the following, if true, contributes to a resolution of the apparent discrepancy described above EXCEPT:

(A) Three-fourths of the Springfield workforce is employed at the same factory outside the city limits.

(B) The average number of cars per household is higher in Springfield than in Rorchester.

(C) Rorchester has fewer railway lines than Springfield.

(D) Buses in Springfield run more frequently and on longer routes than in Rorchester.

(E) Springfield has a larger population than Rorchester does.

9. People who need to reduce their intake of fat and to consume fewer calories often turn to fat substitutes, especially those with zero calories such as N5. But studies indicate that N5 is of no use to such people. Subjects who ate foods prepared with N5 almost invariably reported feeling hungrier afterwards than after eating foods prepared with real fat and consequently they ate more, quickly making up for the calories initially saved by using N5.

The reasoning in the argument is most vulnerable to criticism on the grounds that the argument fails to consider the possibility that

(A) many foods cannot be prepared with N5

(B) N5 has mild but unpleasant side effects

(C) not everyone who eats foods prepared with N5 pays attention to caloric intake

(D) people who know N5 contains zero calories tend to eat more foods prepared with N5 than do people who are unaware that N5 is calorie-free

(E) the total fat intake of people who eat foods prepared with N5 tends to decrease even if their caloric intake does not

10. Music historian: Some critics lament the fact that impoverished postwar recording studios forced early bebop musicians to record extremely short solos, thus leaving a misleading record of their music. But these musicians' beautifully concise playing makes the recordings superb artistic works instead of mere representations of their live solos. Furthermore, the conciseness characteristic of early bebop musicians' recordings fostered a compactness in their subsequent live playing, which the playing of the next generation lacks.

The music historian's statements, if true, most strongly support which one of the following?

(A) Representations of live solos generally are not valuable artistic works.

(B) The difficult postwar recording conditions had some beneficial consequences for bebop.

(C) Short bebop recordings are always superior to longer ones.

(D) The music of the generation immediately following early bebop is of lower overall quality than early bebop.

(E) Musicians will not record extremely short solos unless difficult recording conditions force them to do so.

GO ON TO THE NEXT PAGE.

11. Recent studies indicate a correlation between damage to human chromosome number six and adult schizophrenia. We know, however, that there are people without damage to this chromosome who develop adult schizophrenia and that some people with damage to chromosome number six do not develop adult schizophrenia. So there is no causal connection between damage to human chromosome number six and adult schizophrenia.

Which one of the following most accurately describes a reasoning flaw in the argument above?

(A) The argument ignores the possibility that some but not all types of damage to chromosome number six lead to schizophrenia.
(B) The argument presumes, without providing evidence, that schizophrenia is caused solely by chromosomal damage.
(C) The argument makes a generalization based on an unrepresentative sample population.
(D) The argument mistakes a cause for an effect.
(E) The argument presumes, without providing warrant, that correlation implies causation.

12. City councilperson: Many city residents oppose the city art commission's proposed purchase of an unusual stone edifice, on the grounds that art critics are divided over whether the edifice really qualifies as art. But I argue that the purpose of art is to cause experts to debate ideas, including ideas about what constitutes art itself. Since the edifice has caused experts to debate what constitutes art itself, it does qualify as art.

Which one of the following, if assumed, enables the conclusion of the city councilperson's argument to be properly inferred?

(A) Nothing qualifies as art unless it causes debate among experts.
(B) If an object causes debate among experts, no expert can be certain whether that object qualifies as art.
(C) The purchase of an object that fulfills the purpose of art should not be opposed.
(D) Any object that fulfills the purpose of art qualifies as art.
(E) The city art commission should purchase the edifice if it qualifies as art.

13. It is a given that to be an intriguing person, one must be able to inspire the perpetual curiosity of others. Constantly broadening one's abilities and extending one's intellectual reach will enable one to inspire that curiosity. For such a perpetual expansion of one's mind makes it impossible to be fully comprehended, making one a constant mystery to others.

Which one of the following most accurately expresses the conclusion drawn in the argument above?

(A) To be an intriguing person, one must be able to inspire the perpetual curiosity of others.
(B) If one constantly broadens one's abilities and extends one's intellectual reach, one will be able to inspire the perpetual curiosity of others.
(C) If one's mind becomes impossible to fully comprehend, one will always be a mystery to others.
(D) To inspire the perpetual curiosity of others, one must constantly broaden one's abilities and extend one's intellectual reach.
(E) If one constantly broadens one's abilities and extends one's intellectual reach, one will always have curiosity.

14. Theater managers will not rent a film if they do not believe it will generate enough total revenue—including food-and-beverage concession revenue—to yield a profit. Therefore, since film producers want their films to be shown as widely as possible, they tend to make films that theater managers consider attractive to younger audiences.

Which one of the following is an assumption required by the argument?

(A) Adults consume less of the sort of foods and beverages sold at movie concession stands than do either children or adolescents.
(B) Movies of the kinds that appeal to younger audiences almost never also appeal to older audiences.
(C) Food-and-beverage concession stands in movie theaters are usually more profitable than the movies that are shown.
(D) Theater managers generally believe that a film that is attractive to younger audiences is more likely to be profitable than other films.
(E) Films that have an appeal to older audiences almost never generate a profit for theaters that show them.

GO ON TO THE NEXT PAGE.

15. Almost all advances in genetic research give rise to ethical dilemmas. Government is the exclusive source of funding for most genetic research; those projects not funded by government are funded solely by corporations. One or the other of these sources of funding is necessary for any genetic research.

If all the statements above are true, then which one of the following must be true?

(A) Most advances in genetic research occur in projects funded by government rather than by corporations.
(B) Most genetic research funded by government results in advances that give rise to ethical dilemmas.
(C) At least some advances in genetic research occur in projects funded by corporations.
(D) No ethical dilemmas resulting from advances in genetic research arise without government or corporate funding.
(E) As long as government continues to fund genetic research, that research will give rise to ethical dilemmas.

16. Corporate businesses, like species, must adapt to survive. Businesses that are no longer efficient will become extinct. But sometimes a business cannot adapt without changing its core corporate philosophy. Hence, sometimes a business can survive only by becoming a different corporation.

Which one of the following is an assumption required by the argument?

(A) No business can survive without changing its core corporate philosophy.
(B) As a business becomes less efficient, it invariably surrenders its core corporate philosophy.
(C) Different corporations have different core corporate philosophies.
(D) If a business keeps its core corporate philosophy intact, it will continue to exist.
(E) A business cannot change its core corporate philosophy without becoming a different corporation.

17. A survey taken ten years ago of residents of area L showed that although living conditions were slightly below their country's average, most residents of L reported general satisfaction with their living conditions. However, this year the same survey found that while living conditions are now about the same as the national average, most residents of L report general dissatisfaction with their living conditions.

Which one of the following, if true, would most help to resolve the apparent conflict between the results of the surveys described above?

(A) Residents of area L typically value aspects of living conditions different from the aspects of living conditions that are valued by residents of adjacent areas.
(B) Between the times that the two surveys were conducted, the average living conditions in L's country had substantially declined.
(C) Optimal living conditions were established in the survey by taking into account governmental policies and public demands on three continents.
(D) Living conditions in an area generally improve only if residents perceive their situation as somehow in need of improvement.
(E) Ten years ago the residents of area L were not aware that their living conditions were below the national average.

GO ON TO THE NEXT PAGE.

18. Travel agent: Although most low-fare airlines have had few, if any, accidents, very few such airlines have been in existence long enough for their safety records to be reliably established. Major airlines, on the other hand, usually have long-standing records reliably indicating their degree of safety. Hence, passengers are safer on a major airline than on one of the newer low-fare airlines.

Of the following, which one is the criticism to which the reasoning in the travel agent's argument is most vulnerable?

(A) The argument fails to address adequately the possibility that the average major airline has had a total number of accidents as great as the average low-fare airline has had.

(B) The argument draws a general conclusion about how safe passengers are on different airlines on the basis of safety records that are each from too brief a period to adequately justify such a conclusion.

(C) The argument fails to consider the possibility that long-standing and reliable records documenting an airline's degree of safety may indicate that the airline is unsafe.

(D) The argument takes for granted that airlines that are the safest are also the most reliable in documenting their safety.

(E) The argument fails to address adequately the possibility that even airlines with long-standing, reliable records indicating their degree of safety are still likely to have one or more accidents.

19. Economist: Our economy's weakness is the direct result of consumers' continued reluctance to spend, which in turn is caused by factors such as high-priced goods and services. This reluctance is exacerbated by the fact that the average income is significantly lower than it was five years ago. Thus, even though it is not a perfect solution, if the government were to lower income taxes, the economy would improve.

Which one of the following is an assumption required by the economist's argument?

(A) Increasing consumer spending will cause prices for goods and services to decrease.

(B) If consumer spending increases, the average income will increase.

(C) If income taxes are not lowered, consumers' wages will decline even further.

(D) Consumers will be less reluctant to spend money if income taxes are lowered.

(E) Lowering income taxes will have no effect on government spending.

20. A person with a type B lipid profile is at much greater risk of heart disease than a person with a type A lipid profile. In an experiment, both type A volunteers and type B volunteers were put on a low-fat diet. The cholesterol levels of the type B volunteers soon dropped substantially, although their lipid profiles were unchanged. The type A volunteers, however, showed no benefit from the diet, and 40 percent of them actually shifted to type B profiles.

If the information above is true, which one of the following must also be true?

(A) In the experiment, most of the volunteers had their risk of heart disease reduced at least marginally as a result of having been put on the diet.

(B) People with type B lipid profiles have higher cholesterol levels, on average, than do people with type A lipid profiles.

(C) Apart from adopting the low-fat diet, most of the volunteers did not substantially change any aspect of their lifestyle that would have affected their cholesterol levels or lipid profiles.

(D) The reduction in cholesterol levels in the volunteers is solely responsible for the change in their lipid profiles.

(E) For at least some of the volunteers in the experiment, the risk of heart disease increased after having been put on the low-fat diet.

GO ON TO THE NEXT PAGE.

21. Columnist: Although there is and should be complete freedom of thought and expression, that does not mean that there is nothing wrong with exploiting depraved popular tastes for the sake of financial gain.

Which one of the following judgments conforms most closely to the principle cited by the columnist?

(A) The government should grant artists the right to create whatever works of art they want to create so long as no one considers those works to be depraved.

(B) People who produce depraved movies have the freedom to do so, but that means that they also have the freedom to refrain from doing so.

(C) There should be no laws restricting what books are published, but publishing books that pander to people with depraved tastes is not thereby morally acceptable.

(D) The public has the freedom to purchase whatever recordings are produced, but that does not mean that the government may not limit the production of recordings deemed to be depraved.

(E) One who advocates complete freedom of speech should not criticize others for saying things that he or she believes to exhibit depraved tastes.

22. When a society undergoes slow change, its younger members find great value in the advice of its older members. But when a society undergoes rapid change, young people think that little in the experience of their elders is relevant to them, and so do not value their advice. Thus, we may measure the rate at which a society is changing by measuring the amount of deference its younger members show to their elders.

Which one of the following is an assumption on which the argument depends?

(A) A society's younger members can often accurately discern whether that society is changing rapidly.

(B) How much deference young people show to their elders depends on how much of the elders' experience is practically useful to them.

(C) The deference young people show to their elders varies according to how much the young value their elders' advice.

(D) The faster a society changes, the less relevant the experience of older members of the society is to younger members.

(E) Young people value their elders' advice just insofar as the elders' experience is practically useful to them.

23. Politician: We should impose a tariff on imported fruit to make it cost consumers more than domestic fruit. Otherwise, growers from other countries who can grow better fruit more cheaply will put domestic fruit growers out of business. This will result in farmland's being converted to more lucrative industrial uses and the consequent vanishing of a unique way of life.

The politician's recommendation most closely conforms to which one of the following principles?

(A) A country should put its own economic interest over that of other countries.

(B) The interests of producers should always take precedence over those of consumers.

(C) Social concerns should sometimes take precedence over economic efficiency.

(D) A country should put the interests of its own citizens ahead of those of citizens of other countries.

(E) Government intervention sometimes creates more economic efficiency than free markets.

24. The Kiffer Forest Preserve, in the northernmost part of the Abbimac Valley, is where most of the bears in the valley reside. During the eight years that the main road through the preserve has been closed the preserve's bear population has nearly doubled. Thus, the valley's bear population will increase if the road is kept closed.

Which one of the following, if true, most undermines the argument?

(A) Most of the increase in the preserve's bear population over the past eight years is due to migration.

(B) Only some of the increase in the preserve's bear population over the past eight years is due to migration of bears from other parts of the Abbimac Valley.

(C) Only some of the increase in the preserve's bear population over the past eight years is due to migration of bears from outside the Abbimac Valley.

(D) The bear population in areas of the Abbimac Valley outside the Kiffer Forest Preserve has decreased over the past eight years.

(E) The bear population in the Abbimac Valley has remained about the same over the past eight years.

GO ON TO THE NEXT PAGE.

25. If a wig has any handmade components, it is more expensive than one with none. Similarly, a made-to-measure wig ranges from medium-priced to expensive. Handmade foundations are never found on wigs that do not use human hair. Furthermore, any wig that contains human hair should be dry-cleaned. So all made-to-measure wigs should be dry-cleaned.

The conclusion of the argument follows logically if which one of the following is assumed?

(A) Any wig whose price falls in the medium-priced to expensive range has a handmade foundation.
(B) If a wig's foundation is handmade, then it is more expensive than one whose foundation is not handmade.
(C) A wig that has any handmade components should be dry-cleaned.
(D) If a wig's foundation is handmade, then its price is at least in the medium range.
(E) Any wig that should be dry-cleaned has a foundation that is handmade.

26. Philosopher: Wolves do not tolerate an attack by one wolf on another if the latter wolf demonstrates submission by baring its throat. The same is true of foxes and domesticated dogs. So it would be erroneous to deny that animals have rights on the grounds that only human beings are capable of obeying moral rules.

The philosopher's argument proceeds by attempting to

(A) provide counterexamples to refute a premise on which a particular conclusion is based
(B) establish inductively that all animals possess some form of morality
(C) cast doubt on the principle that being capable of obeying moral rules is a necessary condition for having rights
(D) establish a claim by showing that the denial of that claim entails a logical contradiction
(E) provide evidence suggesting that the concept of morality is often applied too broadly

S T O P

IF YOU FINISH BEFORE TIME IS CALLED, YOU MAY CHECK YOUR WORK ON THIS SECTION ONLY.
DO NOT WORK ON ANY OTHER SECTION IN THE TEST.

SECTION II

Time—35 minutes

27 Questions

Directions: Each set of questions in this section is based on a single passage or a pair of passages. The questions are to be answered on the basis of what is stated or implied in the passage or pair of passages. For some of the questions, more than one of the choices could conceivably answer the question. However, you are to choose the best answer; that is, the response that most accurately and completely answers the question, and blacken the corresponding space on your answer sheet.

Traditional sources of evidence about ancient history are archaeological remains and surviving texts. Those investigating the crafts practiced by women in ancient times, however, often derive little information
(5) from these sources, and the archaeological record is particularly unavailing for the study of ancient textile production, as researchers are thwarted by the perishable nature of cloth. What shreds persisted through millennia were, until recently, often discarded
(10) by excavators as useless, as were loom weights, which appeared to be nothing more than blobs of clay. Ancient texts, meanwhile, rarely mention the creation of textiles; moreover, those references that do exist use archaic, unrevealing terminology. Yet despite these
(15) obstacles, researchers have learned a great deal about ancient textiles and those who made them, and also about how to piece together a whole picture from many disparate sources of evidence.

Technological advances in the analysis of
(20) archaeological remains provide much more information than was previously available, especially about minute remains. Successful modern methods include radiocarbon dating, infrared photography for seeing through dirt without removing it, isotope
(25) "fingerprinting" for tracing sources of raw materials, and thin-layer chromatography for analyzing dyes. As if in preparation for such advances, the field of archaeology has also undergone an important philosophical revolution in the past century. Once little
(30) more than a self-serving quest for artifacts to stock museums and private collections, the field has transformed itself into a scientific pursuit of knowledge about past cultures. As part of this process, archaeologists adopted the fundamental precept of
(35) preserving all objects, even those that have no immediately discernible value. Thus in the 1970s two researchers found the oldest known complete garment, a 5,000-year-old linen shirt, among a tumbled heap of dirty linens that had been preserved as part of the well-
(40) known Petrie collection decades before anyone began to study the history of textiles.

The history of textiles and of the craftswomen who produced them has also advanced on a different front: recreating the actual production of cloth.
(45) Reconstructing and implementing ancient production methods provides a valuable way of generating and checking hypotheses. For example, these techniques made it possible to confirm that the excavated pieces of clay once considered useless in fact functioned as loom
(50) weights. Similarly, scholars have until recently been

obliged to speculate as to which one of two statues of Athena, one large and one small, was adorned with a dress created by a group of Athenian women for a festival, as described in surviving texts. Because
(55) records show that it took nine months to produce the dress, scholars assumed it must have adorned the large statue. But by investigating the methods of production and the size of the looms used, researchers have ascertained that in fact a dress for the small statue
(60) would have taken nine months to produce.

1. Which one of the following most accurately expresses the main point of the passage?

(A) Archaeology is an expanding discipline that has transformed itself in response both to scientific advances and to changing cultural demands such as a recently increasing interest in women's history.

(B) A diversity of new approaches to the study of ancient textiles has enabled researchers to infer much about the history of textiles and their creators in the ancient world from the scant evidence that remains.

(C) Despite many obstacles, research into the textile production methods used by women in the ancient world has advanced over the past century to the point that archaeologists can now replicate ancient equipment and production techniques.

(D) Research into the history of textiles has spurred sweeping changes in the field of archaeology, from the application of advanced technology to the revaluation of ancient artifacts that were once deemed useless.

(E) Though researchers have verified certain theories about the history of textiles by using technological developments such as radiocarbon dating, most significant findings in this field have grown out of the reconstruction of ancient production techniques.

GO ON TO THE NEXT PAGE.

2. The author's attitude concerning the history of ancient textile production can most accurately be described as

(A) skeptical regarding the validity of some of the new hypotheses proposed by researchers

(B) doubtful that any additional useful knowledge can be generated given the nature of the evidence available

(C) impatient about the pace of research in light of the resources available

(D) optimistic that recent scholarly advances will attract increasing numbers of researchers

(E) satisfied that considerable progress is being made in this field

3. The passage indicates that the re-creation of ancient techniques was used in which one of the following?

(A) investigating the meanings of certain previously unintelligible technical terms in ancient texts

(B) tracing the sources of raw materials used in the production of certain fabrics

(C) constructing certain public museum displays concerning cloth-making

(D) verifying that a particular 5,000-year-old cloth was indeed a shirt

(E) exploring the issue of which of two statues of Athena was clothed with a particular garment

4. The author intends the term "traditional sources" (line 1) to exclude which one of the following?

(A) ancient clay objects that cannot be identified as pieces of pottery by the researchers who unearth them

(B) historically significant pieces of cloth discovered in the course of an excavation

(C) the oldest known complete garment, which was found among other pieces of cloth in a collection

(D) re-creations of looms from which inferences about ancient weaving techniques can be made

(E) ancient accounts of the adornment of a statue of Athena with a dress made by Athenian women

5. The passage as a whole functions primarily as

(A) a defense of the controversial methods adopted by certain researchers in a particular discipline

(B) a set of recommendations to guide future activities in a particular field of inquiry

(C) an account of how a particular branch of research has successfully coped with certain difficulties

(D) a rejection of some commonly held views about the methodologies of a certain discipline

(E) a summary of the hypotheses advanced by researchers who have used innovative methods of investigation

6. According to the passage, which one of the following was an element in the transformation of archaeology in the past century?

(A) an increased interest in the crafts practiced in the ancient world

(B) some archaeologists' adoption of textile conservation experts' preservation techniques

(C) innovative methods of restoring damaged artifacts

(D) the discovery of the oldest known complete garment

(E) archaeologists' policy of not discarding ancient objects that have no readily identifiable value

7. Which one of the following most accurately describes the function of the first paragraph in relation to the rest of the passage?

(A) A particularly difficult archaeological problem is described in order to underscore the significance of new methods used to resolve that problem, which are described in the following paragraphs.

(B) A previously neglected body of archaeological evidence is described in order to cast doubt on received views regarding ancient cultures developed from conventional sources of evidence, as described in the following paragraphs.

(C) The fruitfulness of new technologically based methods of analysis is described in order to support the subsequent argument that apparently insignificant archaeological remains ought to be preserved for possible future research.

(D) The findings of recent archaeological research are outlined as the foundation for a claim advanced in the following paragraphs that the role of women in ancient cultures has been underestimated by archaeologists.

(E) A recently developed branch of archaeological research is described as evidence for the subsequent argument that other, more established branches of archaeology should take advantage of new technologies in their research.

GO ON TO THE NEXT PAGE.

This passage was adapted from articles published in the 1990s.

The success that Nigerian-born computer scientist Philip Emeagwali (b. 1954) has had in designing computers that solve real-world problems has been fueled by his willingness to reach beyond established
(5) paradigms and draw inspiration for his designs from nature. In the 1980s, Emeagwali achieved breakthroughs in the design of parallel computer systems. Whereas single computers work sequentially, making one calculation at a time, computers
(10) connected in parallel can process calculations simultaneously. In 1989, Emeagwali pioneered the use of massively parallel computers that used a network of thousands of smaller computers to solve what is considered one of the most computationally difficult
(15) problems: predicting the flow of oil through the subterranean geologic formations that make up oil fields. Until that time, supercomputers had been used for oil field calculations, but because these supercomputers worked sequentially, they were too
(20) slow and inefficient to accurately predict such extremely complex movements.

To model oil field flow using a computer requires the simulation of the distribution of the oil at tens of thousands of locations throughout the field. At each
(25) location, hundreds of simultaneous calculations must be made at regular time intervals relating to such variables as temperature, direction of oil flow, viscosity, and pressure, as well as geologic properties of the basin holding the oil. In order to solve this
(30) problem, Emeagwali designed a massively parallel computer by using the Internet to connect to more than 65,000 smaller computers. One of the great difficulties of parallel computing is dividing up the tasks among the separate smaller computers so that
(35) they do not interfere with each other, and it was here that Emeagwali turned to natural processes for ideas, noting that tree species that survive today are those that, over the course of hundreds of millions of years, have developed branching patterns that have
(40) maximized the amount of sunlight gathered and the quantity of water and sap delivered. Emeagwali demonstrated that, for modeling certain phenomena such as subterranean oil flow, a network design based on the mathematical principle that underlies the
(45) branching structures of trees will enable a massively parallel computer to gather and broadcast the largest quantity of messages to its processing points in the shortest time.

In 1996 Emeagwali had another breakthrough
(50) when he presented the design for a massively parallel computer that he claims will be powerful enough to predict global weather patterns a century in advance. The computer's design is based on the geometry of bees' honeycombs, which use an extremely efficient

(55) three-dimensional spacing. Emeagwali believes that computer scientists in the future will increasingly look to nature for elegant solutions to complex technical problems. This paradigm shift, he asserts, will enable us to better understand the systems
(60) evolved by nature and, thereby, to facilitate the evolution of human technology.

8. Which one of the following most accurately expresses the main point of the passage?

(A)   Emeagwali's establishment of new computational paradigms has enabled parallel computer systems to solve a wide array of real-world problems that supercomputers cannot solve.

(B)   Emeagwali has shown that scientists' allegiance to established paradigms has until now prevented the solution of many real-world computational problems that could otherwise have been solved with little difficulty.

(C)   Emeagwali's discovery of the basic mathematical principles underlying natural systems has led to a growing use of parallel computer systems to solve complex real-world computational problems.

(D)   Emeagwali has designed parallel computer systems that are modeled on natural systems and that are aimed at solving real-world computational problems that would be difficult to solve with more traditional designs.

(E)   The paradigm shift initiated by Emeagwali's computer designs has made it more likely that scientists will in the future look to systems evolved by nature to facilitate the evolution of human technology.

GO ON TO THE NEXT PAGE.

9. According to the passage, which one of the following is true?

(A) Emeagwali's breakthroughs in computer design have begun to make computers that work sequentially obsolete.

(B) Emeagwali's first breakthrough in computer design came in response to a request by an oil company.

(C) Emeagwali was the first to use a massively parallel computer to predict the flow of oil in oil fields.

(D) Emeagwali was the first computer scientist to use nature as a model for human technology.

(E) Emeagwali was the first to apply parallel processing to solving real-world problems.

10. The passage most strongly suggests that Emeagwali holds which one of the following views?

(A) Some natural systems have arrived at efficient solutions to problems that are analogous in significant ways to technical problems faced by computer scientists.

(B) Global weather is likely too complicated to be accurately predictable more than a few decades in advance.

(C) Most computer designs will in the future be inspired by natural systems.

(D) Massively parallel computers will eventually be practical enough to warrant their use even in relatively mundane computing tasks.

(E) The mathematical structure of branching trees is useful primarily for designing computer systems to predict the flow of oil through oil fields.

11. Which one of the following most accurately describes the function of the first two sentences of the second paragraph?

(A) They provide an example of an established paradigm that Emeagwali's work has challenged.

(B) They help explain why supercomputers are unable to accurately predict the movements of oil through underground geologic formations.

(C) They provide examples of a network design based on the mathematical principles underlying the branching structures of trees.

(D) They describe a mathematical model that Emeagwali used in order to understand a natural system.

(E) They provide specific examples of a paradigm shift that will help scientists understand certain systems evolved by nature.

12. Which one of the following, if true, would provide the most support for Emeagwali's prediction mentioned in lines 55–58?

(A) Until recently, computer scientists have had very limited awareness of many of the mathematical principles that have been shown to underlie a wide variety of natural processes.

(B) Some of the variables affecting global weather patterns have yet to be discovered by scientists who study these patterns.

(C) Computer designs for the prediction of natural phenomena tend to be more successful when those phenomena are not affected by human activities.

(D) Some of the mathematical principles underlying Emeagwali's model of oil field flow also underlie his designs for other massively parallel computer systems.

(E) Underlying the designs for many traditional technologies are mathematical principles of which the designers of those technologies were not explicitly aware.

13. It can be inferred from the passage that one of the reasons massively parallel computers had not been used to model oil field flow prior to 1989 is that

(A) supercomputers are sufficiently powerful to handle most computational problems, including most problems arising from oil production

(B) the possibility of using a network of smaller computers to solve computationally difficult problems had not yet been considered

(C) the general public was not yet aware of the existence or vast capabilities of the Internet

(D) oil companies had not yet perceived the need for modeling the flow of oil in subterranean fields

(E) smaller computers can interfere with one another when they are connected together in parallel to solve a computationally difficult problem

GO ON TO THE NEXT PAGE.

Proponents of the tangible-object theory of copyright argue that copyright and similar intellectual-property rights can be explained as logical extensions of the right to own concrete, tangible objects. This
(5) view depends on the claim that every copyrightable work can be manifested in some physical form, such as a manuscript or a videotape. It also accepts the premise that ownership of an object confers a number of rights on the owner, who may essentially do whatever he or
(10) she pleases with the object to the extent that this does not violate other people's rights. One may, for example, hide or display the object, copy it, or destroy it. One may also transfer ownership of it to another.

In creating a new and original object from
(15) materials that one owns, one becomes the owner of that object and thereby acquires all of the rights that ownership entails. But if the owner transfers ownership of the object, the full complement of rights is not necessarily transferred to the new owner; instead, the
(20) original owner may retain one or more of these rights. This notion of retained rights is common in many areas of law; for example, the seller of a piece of land may retain certain rights to the land in the form of easements or building restrictions. Applying the notion
(25) of retained rights to the domain of intellectual property, theorists argue that copyrighting a work secures official recognition of one's intention to retain certain rights to that work. Among the rights typically retained by the original producer of an object such as a literary
(30) manuscript or a musical score would be the right to copy the object for profit and the right to use it as a guide for the production of similar or analogous things—for example, a public performance of a musical score.
(35) According to proponents of the tangible-object theory, its chief advantage is that it justifies intellectual property rights without recourse to the widely accepted but problematic supposition that one can own abstract, intangible things such as ideas. But while this account
(40) seems plausible for copyrightable entities that do, in fact, have enduring tangible forms, it cannot accommodate the standard assumption that such evanescent things as live broadcasts of sporting events can be copyrighted. More importantly, it does not
(45) acknowledge that in many cases the work of conceiving ideas is more crucial and more valuable than that of putting them into tangible form. Suppose that a poet dictates a new poem to a friend, who writes it down on paper that the friend has supplied. The
(50) creator of the tangible object in this case is not the poet but the friend, and there would seem to be no ground for the poet's claiming copyright unless the poet can be said to already own the ideas expressed in the work.

14. Which one of the following most accurately expresses the main point of the passage?

(A) Copyright and other intellectual-property rights can be explained as logical extensions of the right to own concrete objects.

(B) Attempts to explain copyright and similar intellectual-property rights purely in terms of rights to ownership of physical objects are ultimately misguided.

(C) Copyrighting a work amounts to securing official recognition of one's intention to retain certain rights to that work.

(D) Explanations of copyright and other intellectual-property rights in terms of rights to ownership of tangible objects fail to consider the argument that ideas should be allowed to circulate freely.

(E) Under the tangible-object theory of intellectual property, rights of ownership are straightforwardly applicable to both ideas and physical objects.

15. According to the passage, the theory that copyright and other intellectual-property rights can be construed as logical extensions of the right to own concrete, tangible objects depends on the claim that

(A) any work entitled to intellectual-property protection can be expressed in physical form

(B) only the original creator of an intellectual work can hold the copyright for that work

(C) the work of putting ideas into tangible form is more crucial and more valuable than the work of conceiving those ideas

(D) in a few cases, it is necessary to recognize the right to own abstract, intangible things

(E) the owner of an item of intellectual property may legally destroy it

16. The passage most directly answers which one of the following questions?

(A) Do proponents of the tangible-object theory of intellectual property advocate any changes in existing laws relating to copyright?

(B) Do proponents of the tangible-object theory of intellectual property hold that ownership of anything besides real estate can involve retained rights?

(C) Has the tangible-object theory of intellectual property influenced the ways in which copyright cases or other cases involving issues of intellectual property are decided in the courts?

(D) Does existing copyright law provide protection against unauthorized copying of manuscripts and musical scores in cases in which their creators have not officially applied for copyright protection?

(E) Are there standard procedures governing the transfer of intellectual property that are common to most legal systems?

17. Suppose an inventor describes an innovative idea for an invention to an engineer, who volunteers to draft specifications for a prototype and then produces the prototype using the engineer's own materials. Which one of the following statements would apply to this case under the tangible-object theory of intellectual property, as the author describes that theory?

(A) Only the engineer is entitled to claim the invention as intellectual property.
(B) Only the inventor is entitled to claim the invention as intellectual property.
(C) The inventor and the engineer are equally entitled to claim the invention as intellectual property.
(D) The engineer is entitled to claim the invention as intellectual property, but only if the inventor retains the right to all profits generated by the invention.
(E) The inventor is entitled to claim the invention as intellectual property, but only if the engineer retains the right to all profits generated by the invention.

18. Legal theorists supporting the tangible-object theory of intellectual property are most likely to believe which one of the following?

(A) A literary work cannot receive copyright protection unless it exists in an edition produced by an established publisher.
(B) Most legal systems explicitly rely on the tangible-object theory of intellectual property in order to avoid asserting that one can own abstract things.
(C) Copyright protects the right to copy for profit, but not the right to copy for other reasons.
(D) Some works deserving of copyright protection simply cannot be manifested as concrete, tangible objects.
(E) To afford patent protection for inventions, the law need not invoke the notion of inventors' ownership of abstract ideas.

19. The passage provides the most support for inferring which one of the following statements?

(A) In most transactions involving the transfer of non-intellectual property, at least some rights of ownership are retained by the seller.
(B) The notion of retained rights of ownership is currently applied to only those areas of law that do not involve intellectual property.
(C) The idea that ownership of the right to copy an item for profit can be transferred is compatible with a tangible-object theory of intellectual property.
(D) Ownership of intellectual property is sufficiently protected by the provisions that, under many legal systems, apply to ownership of material things such as land.
(E) Protection of computer programs under intellectual-property law is justifiable only if the programs are likely to be used as a guide for the production of similar or analogous programs.

20. It can be inferred that the author of the passage is most likely to believe which one of the following?

(A) Theorists who suggest that the notion of retained rights is applicable to intellectual property do not fully understand what it means to transfer ownership of property.
(B) If a work does not exist in a concrete, tangible form, there is no valid theoretical basis for claiming that it should have copyright protection.
(C) Under existing statutes, creators of original tangible works that have intellectual or artistic significance generally do not have the legal right to own the abstract ideas embodied in those works.
(D) An adequate theoretical justification of copyright would likely presuppose that a work's creator originally owns the ideas embodied in that work.
(E) It is common, but incorrect, to assume that such evanescent things as live broadcasts of sporting events can be copyrighted.

GO ON TO THE NEXT PAGE.

Passage A

In music, a certain complexity of sounds can be expected to have a positive effect on the listener. A single, pure tone is not that interesting to explore; a measure of intricacy is required to excite human
(5) curiosity. Sounds that are too complex or disorganized, however, tend to be overwhelming. We prefer some sort of coherence, a principle that connects the various sounds and makes them comprehensible.

In this respect, music is like human language.
(10) Single sounds are in most cases not sufficient to convey meaning in speech, whereas when put together in a sequence they form words and sentences. Likewise, if the tones in music are not perceived to be tied together sequentially or rhythmically—for
(15) example, in what is commonly called melody— listeners are less likely to feel any emotional connection or to show appreciation.

Certain music can also have a relaxing effect. The fact that such music tends to be continuous and
(20) rhythmical suggests a possible explanation for this effect. In a natural environment, danger tends to be accompanied by sudden, unexpected sounds. Thus, a background of constant noise suggests peaceful conditions; discontinuous sounds demand more
(25) attention. Even soft discontinuous sounds that we consciously realize do not signal danger can be disturbing—for example, the erratic dripping of a leaky tap. A continuous sound, particularly one that is judged to be safe, relaxes the brain.

Passage B

(30) There are certain elements within music, such as a change of melodic line or rhythm, that create expectations about the future development of the music. The expectation the listener has about the further course of musical events is a key determinant
(35) for the experience of "musical emotions." Music creates expectations that, if not immediately satisfied, create tension. Emotion is experienced in relation to the buildup and release of tension. The more elaborate the buildup of tension, the more intense the emotions
(40) that will be experienced. When resolution occurs, relaxation follows.

The interruption of the expected musical course, depending on one's personal involvement, causes the search for an explanation. This results from a
(45) "mismatch" between one's musical expectation and the actual course of the music. Negative emotions will be the result of an extreme mismatch between expectations and experience. Positive emotions result if the converse happens.

(50) When we listen to music, we take into account factors such as the complexity and novelty of the music. The degree to which the music sounds familiar determines whether the music is experienced as pleasurable or uncomfortable. The pleasure
(55) experienced is minimal when the music is entirely new to the listener, increases with increasing familiarity, and decreases again when the music is totally known.

Musical preference is based on one's desire to maintain a constant level of certain preferable
(60) emotions. As such, a trained listener will have a greater preference for complex melodies than will a naive listener, as the threshold for experiencing emotion is higher.

21. Which one of the following concepts is linked to positive musical experiences in both passages?

    (A) continuous sound
    (B) tension
    (C) language
    (D) improvisation
    (E) complexity

22. The passages most strongly suggest that both are targeting an audience that is interested in which one of the following?

    (A) the theoretical underpinnings of how music is composed
    (B) the nature of the conceptual difference between music and discontinuous sound
    (C) the impact music can have on human emotional states
    (D) the most effective techniques for teaching novices to appreciate complex music
    (E) the influence music has had on the development of spoken language

23. Which one of the following describes a preference that is most analogous to the preference mentioned in the first paragraph of passage A?

    (A) the preference of some people for falling asleep to white noise, such as the sound of an electric fan
    (B) the preference of many moviegoers for movies with plots that are clear and easy to follow
    (C) the preference of many diners for restaurants that serve large portions
    (D) the preference of many young listeners for fast music over slower music
    (E) the preference of most children for sweet foods over bitter foods

GO ON TO THE NEXT PAGE.

24. Which one of the following most accurately expresses the main point of passage B?

 (A) The type of musical emotion experienced by a listener is determined by the level to which the listener's expectations are satisfied.

 (B) Trained listeners are more able to consciously manipulate their own emotional experiences of complex music than are naive listeners.

 (C) If the development of a piece of music is greatly at odds with the listener's musical expectations, then the listener will experience negative emotions.

 (D) Listeners can learn to appreciate changes in melodic line and other musical complexities.

 (E) Music that is experienced by listeners as relaxing usually produces a buildup and release of tension in those listeners.

25. Which one of the following most undermines the explanation provided in passage A for the relaxing effect that some music has on listeners?

 (A) The musical traditions of different cultures vary greatly in terms of the complexity of the rhythms they employ.

 (B) The rhythmic structure of a language is determined in part by the pattern of stressed syllables in the words and sentences of the language.

 (C) Many people find the steady and rhythmic sound of a rocking chair to be very unnerving.

 (D) The sudden interruption of the expected development of a melody tends to interfere with listeners' perception of the melody as coherent.

 (E) Some of the most admired contemporary composers write music that is notably simpler than is most of the music written in previous centuries.

26. Which one of the following would be most appropriate as a title for each of the passages?

 (A) "The Biological Underpinnings of Musical Emotions"

 (B) "The Psychology of Listener Response to Music"

 (C) "How Music Differs from Other Art Forms"

 (D) "Cultural Patterns in Listeners' Responses to Music"

 (E) "How Composers Convey Meaning Through Music"

27. It can be inferred that both authors would be likely to agree with which one of the following statements?

 (A) The more complex a piece of music, the more it is likely to be enjoyed by most listeners.

 (B) More knowledgeable listeners tend to prefer music that is discontinuous and unpredictable.

 (C) The capacity of music to elicit strong emotional responses from listeners is the central determinant of its artistic value.

 (D) Music that lacks a predictable course is unlikely to cause a listener to feel relaxed.

 (E) Music that changes from soft to loud is perceived as disturbing and unpleasant by most listeners.

S T O P

IF YOU FINISH BEFORE TIME IS CALLED, YOU MAY CHECK YOUR WORK ON THIS SECTION ONLY.
DO NOT WORK ON ANY OTHER SECTION IN THE TEST.

SECTION III

Time—35 minutes

23 Questions

Directions: Each group of questions in this section is based on a set of conditions. In answering some of the questions, it may be useful to draw a rough diagram. Choose the response that most accurately and completely answers each question and blacken the corresponding space on your answer sheet.

Questions 1–6

Historical records show that over the course of five consecutive years—601, 602, 603, 604, and 605—a certain emperor began construction of six monuments: F, G, H, L, M, and S. A historian is trying to determine the years in which the individual monuments were begun. The following facts have been established:

L was begun in a later year than G, but in an earlier year than F.

H was begun no earlier than 604.

M was begun earlier than 604.

Two of the monuments were begun in 601, and no other monument was begun in the same year as any of the other monuments.

1. Which one of the following could be an accurate matching of monuments to the years in which they were begun?

(A) 601: G;   602: L, S; 603: M; 604: H; 605: F
(B) 601: G, M; 602: L;   603: H; 604: S; 605: F
(C) 601: G, M; 602: S;   603: F; 604: L; 605: H
(D) 601: G, S; 602: L;   603: F; 604: M; 605: H
(E) 601: G, S; 602: L;   603: M; 604: H; 605: F

2. What is the latest year in which L could have been begun?

(A)   601
(B)   602
(C)   603
(D)   604
(E)   605

3. The years in which each of the monuments were begun can be completely determined if which one of the following is discovered to be true?

(A)   F was begun in 603.
(B)   G was begun in 602.
(C)   H was begun in 605.
(D)   M was begun in 602.
(E)   S was begun in 604.

4. Which one of the following must be true?

(A)   F was begun in a later year than M.
(B)   F was begun in a later year than S.
(C)   H was begun in a later year than F.
(D)   H was begun in a later year than S.
(E)   M was begun in a later year than G.

5. L must be the monument that was begun in 602 if which one of the following is true?

(A)   F was begun in 605.
(B)   G was begun in 601.
(C)   H was begun in 604.
(D)   M was begun in 601.
(E)   S was begun in 603.

6. If M was begun in a later year than L, then which one of the following could be true?

(A)   F was begun in 603.
(B)   G was begun in 602.
(C)   H was begun in 605.
(D)   L was begun in 603.
(E)   S was begun in 604.

GO ON TO THE NEXT PAGE.

Questions 7–12

A company organizing on-site day care consults with a group of parents composed exclusively of volunteers from among the seven employees—Felicia, Leah, Masatomo, Rochelle, Salman, Terry, and Veena—who have become parents this year. The composition of the volunteer group must be consistent with the following:

If Rochelle volunteers, then so does Masatomo.
If Masatomo volunteers, then so does Terry.
If Salman does not volunteer, then Veena volunteers.
If Rochelle does not volunteer, then Leah volunteers.
If Terry volunteers, then neither Felicia nor Veena volunteers.

7. Which one of the following could be a complete and accurate list of the volunteers?

(A) Felicia, Salman
(B) Masatomo, Rochelle
(C) Leah, Salman, Terry
(D) Salman, Rochelle, Veena
(E) Leah, Salman, Terry, Veena

8. If Veena volunteers, then which one of the following could be true?

(A) Felicia and Rochelle also volunteer.
(B) Felicia and Salman also volunteer.
(C) Leah and Masatomo also volunteer.
(D) Leah and Terry also volunteer.
(E) Salman and Terry also volunteer.

9. If Terry does not volunteer, then which one of the following CANNOT be true?

(A) Felicia volunteers.
(B) Leah volunteers.
(C) Rochelle volunteers.
(D) Salman volunteers.
(E) Veena volunteers.

10. If Masatomo volunteers, then which one of the following could be true?

(A) Felicia volunteers.
(B) Leah volunteers.
(C) Veena volunteers.
(D) Salman does not volunteer.
(E) Terry does not volunteer.

11. If Felicia volunteers, then which one of the following must be true?

(A) Leah volunteers.
(B) Salman volunteers.
(C) Veena does not volunteer.
(D) Exactly three of the employees volunteer.
(E) Exactly four of the employees volunteer.

12. Which one of the following pairs of employees is such that at least one member of the pair volunteers?

(A) Felicia and Terry
(B) Leah and Masatomo
(C) Leah and Veena
(D) Rochelle and Salman
(E) Salman and Terry

GO ON TO THE NEXT PAGE.

Questions 13–17

Flyhigh Airlines owns exactly two planes: P and Q.
Getaway Airlines owns exactly three planes: R, S, T. On
Sunday, each plane makes exactly one flight, according to
the following conditions:

Only one plane departs at a time.
Each plane makes either a domestic or an international
 flight, but not both.
Plane P makes an international flight.
Planes Q and R make domestic flights.
All international flights depart before any domestic
 flight.
Any Getaway domestic flight departs before Flyhigh's
 domestic flight.

13. Which one of the following could be the order, from
 first to last, in which the five planes depart?

 (A)   P, Q, R, S, T
 (B)   P, Q, T, S, R
 (C)   P, S, T, Q, R
 (D)   P, S, T, R, Q
 (E)   T, S, R, P, Q

14. The plane that departs second could be any one of
 exactly how many of the planes?

 (A)   one
 (B)   two
 (C)   three
 (D)   four
 (E)   five

15. If plane S departs sometime before plane P, then
 which one of the following must be false?

 (A)   Plane S departs first.
 (B)   Plane S departs third.
 (C)   Plane T departs second.
 (D)   Plane T departs third.
 (E)   Plane T departs fourth.

16. Which one of the following must be true?

 (A)   Plane P departs first.
 (B)   Plane Q departs last.
 (C)   Plane R departs second.
 (D)   Plane S departs first.
 (E)   Plane T departs fourth.

17. If plane S departs third, then each of the following can
 be true EXCEPT:

 (A)   Plane R departs sometime before plane S and
        sometime before plane T.
 (B)   Plane S departs sometime before plane Q and
        sometime before plane T.
 (C)   Plane S departs sometime before plane R and
        sometime before plane T.
 (D)   Plane T departs sometime before plane P and
        sometime before plane S.
 (E)   Plane T departs sometime before plane R and
        sometime before plane S.

GO ON TO THE NEXT PAGE.

Questions 18–23

A student is choosing courses to take during a summer school session. Each summer school student must take at least three courses from among the following seven: history, linguistics, music, physics, statistics, theater, and writing. The summer school schedule restricts the courses a student can take in the following ways:

    If history is taken, then neither statistics nor music can be taken.

    If music is taken, then neither physics nor theater can be taken.

    If writing is taken, then neither physics nor statistics can be taken.

18. The student could take which one of the following groups of courses during the summer school session?

    (A)   history, linguistics, and statistics
    (B)   history, music, and physics
    (C)   history, physics, and theater
    (D)   linguistics, physics, theater, and writing
    (E)   music, theater, and writing

19. What is the maximum number of courses the student could take during the summer school session?

    (A)   seven
    (B)   six
    (C)   five
    (D)   four
    (E)   three

20. If the student takes neither physics nor writing, then it could be true that the student also takes neither

    (A)   history nor linguistics
    (B)   history nor music
    (C)   history nor statistics
    (D)   linguistics nor music
    (E)   statistics nor theater

21. If the student takes music, then which one of the following must the student also take?

    (A)   writing
    (B)   theater
    (C)   statistics
    (D)   physics
    (E)   linguistics

22. The student must take one or the other or both of

    (A)   history or statistics
    (B)   linguistics or theater
    (C)   linguistics or writing
    (D)   music or physics
    (E)   theater or writing

23. Which one of the following, if substituted for the restriction that if music is taken, then neither physics nor theater can be taken, would have the same effect in determining which courses the student can take?

    (A)   If music is taken, then either statistics or writing must also be taken.
    (B)   The only courses that are eligible to be taken together with music are linguistics, statistics, and writing.
    (C)   The only courses that are eligible to be taken together with physics are history and linguistics.
    (D)   The only courses that are eligible to be taken together with theater are history, linguistics, and writing.
    (E)   If both physics and theater are taken, then music cannot be taken.

S T O P

IF YOU FINISH BEFORE TIME IS CALLED, YOU MAY CHECK YOUR WORK ON THIS SECTION ONLY.
DO NOT WORK ON ANY OTHER SECTION IN THE TEST.

SECTION IV

Time—35 minutes

25 Questions

Directions: The questions in this section are based on the reasoning contained in brief statements or passages. For some questions, more than one of the choices could conceivably answer the question. However, you are to choose the best answer; that is, the response that most accurately and completely answers the question. You should not make assumptions that are by commonsense standards implausible, superfluous, or incompatible with the passage. After you have chosen the best answer, blacken the corresponding space on your answer sheet.

1. Automated flight technology can guide an aircraft very reliably, from navigation to landing. Yet this technology, even when functioning correctly, is not a perfect safeguard against human error.

    Which one of the following, if true, most helps to explain the situation described above?

    (A) Automated flight technology does not always function correctly.
    (B) Smaller aircraft do not always have their automated flight technology updated regularly.
    (C) If a plane's automated flight technology malfunctions, crew members have to operate the plane manually.
    (D) Some airplane crashes are due neither to human error nor to malfunction of automated flight technology.
    (E) Automated flight technology invariably executes exactly the commands that humans give it.

2. To keep one's hands warm during the winter, one never needs gloves or mittens. One can always keep one's hands warm simply by putting on an extra layer of clothing, such as a thermal undershirt or a sweater. After all, keeping one's vital organs warm can keep one's hands warm as well.

    Which one of the following, if true, most weakens the argument?

    (A) Maintaining the temperature of your hands is far less important, physiologically, than maintaining the temperature of your torso.
    (B) Several layers of light garments will keep one's vital organs warmer than will one or two heavy garments.
    (C) Wearing an extra layer of clothing will not keep one's hands warm at temperatures low enough to cause frostbite.
    (D) Keeping one's hands warm by putting on an extra layer of clothing is less effective than turning up the heat.
    (E) The physical effort required to put on an extra layer of clothing does not stimulate circulation enough to warm your hands.

3. The reason music with a simple recurring rhythm exerts a strong primordial appeal is that it reminds us of the womb environment. After all, the first sound heard within the womb is the comforting sound of the mother's regular heartbeat. So in taking away from us the warmth and security of the womb, birth also takes away a primal and constant source of comfort. Thus it is extremely natural that in seeking sensations of warmth and security throughout life, people would be strongly drawn toward simple recurring rhythmic sounds.

    Which one of the following most accurately expresses the main conclusion drawn in the reasoning above?

    (A) The explanation of the strong primordial appeal of music with a simple recurring rhythm is that it reminds us of the womb environment.
    (B) The comforting sound of the mother's regular heartbeat is the first sound that is heard inside the womb.
    (C) Birth deprives us of a primal and constant source of comfort when it takes away the warmth and security of the womb.
    (D) People seek sensations of warmth and security throughout life because birth takes away the warmth and security of the womb.
    (E) The comforting sound of the mother's regular heartbeat is a simple recurring rhythmic sound.

GO ON TO THE NEXT PAGE.

4. Linguist: Most people can tell whether a sequence of words in their own dialect is grammatical. Yet few people who can do so are able to specify the relevant grammatical rules.

Which one of the following best illustrates the principle underlying the linguist's statements?

(A) Some people are able to write cogent and accurate narrative descriptions of events. But these people are not necessarily also capable of composing emotionally moving and satisfying poems.

(B) Engineers who apply the principles of physics to design buildings and bridges must know a great deal more than do the physicists who discover these principles.

(C) Some people are able to tell whether any given piece of music is a waltz. But the majority of these people cannot state the defining characteristics of a waltz.

(D) Those travelers who most enjoy their journeys are not always those most capable of vividly describing the details of those journeys to others.

(E) Quite a few people know the rules of chess, but only a small number of them can play chess very well.

5. Company president: For the management consultant position, we shall interview only those applicants who have worked for management consulting firms generally recognized as in the top 1 percent of firms worldwide. When we finally select somebody, then, we can be sure to have selected one of the best management consultants available.

The company president's reasoning is most vulnerable to criticism on the grounds that it

(A) takes for granted that only the best management consultants have worked for the top management consulting firms

(B) generalizes from too small a sample of management consulting firms worldwide

(C) takes for granted that if something is true of each member of a collection, then it is also true of the collection as a whole

(D) presumes, without providing warrant, that persons who have worked for the top companies will accept a job offer

(E) presumes, without providing justification, that highly competent management consultants are highly competent at every task

6. Beginners typically decide each chess move by considering the consequences. Expert players, in contrast, primarily use pattern-recognition techniques. That is, such a player recognizes having been in a similar position before and makes a decision based on information recalled about the consequences of moves chosen on that prior occasion.

Which one of the following is most strongly supported by the information above?

(A) Beginning chess players are better at thinking through the consequences of chess moves than experts are.

(B) A beginning chess player should use pattern-recognition techniques when deciding what move to make.

(C) One's chess skills will improve only if one learns to use pattern-recognition techniques.

(D) In playing chess, an expert player relies crucially on his or her memory.

(E) Any chess player who played other games that require pattern-recognition skills would thereby improve his or her chess skills.

7. Farmer: Because water content is what makes popcorn pop, the kernels must dry at just the right speed to trap the correct amount of water. The best way to achieve this effect is to have the sun dry the corn while the corn is still in the field, but I always dry the ears on a screen in a warm, dry room.

Which one of the following, if true, most helps to resolve the apparent discrepancy between the farmer's theory and practice?

(A) The region in which the farmer grows popcorn experiences a long, cloudy season that begins shortly before the popcorn in fields would begin to dry.

(B) Leaving popcorn to dry on its stalks in the field is the least expensive method of drying it.

(C) Drying popcorn on its stalks in the field is only one of several methods that allow the kernels' water content to reach acceptable levels.

(D) When popcorn does not dry sufficiently, it will still pop, but it will take several minutes to do so, even under optimal popping conditions.

(E) If popcorn is allowed to dry too much, it will not pop.

GO ON TO THE NEXT PAGE.

8. Factory manager: One reason the automobile parts this factory produces are expensive is that our manufacturing equipment is outdated and inefficient. Our products would be more competitively priced if we were to refurbish the factory completely with new, more efficient equipment. Therefore, since to survive in today's market we have to make our products more competitively priced, we must completely refurbish the factory in order to survive.

The reasoning in the factory manager's argument is flawed because this argument

(A) fails to recognize that the price of a particular commodity can change over time
(B) shifts without justification from treating something as one way of achieving a goal to treating it as the only way of achieving that goal
(C) argues that one thing is the cause of another when the evidence given indicates that the second thing may in fact be the cause of the first
(D) recommends a solution to a problem without first considering any possible causes of that problem
(E) fails to make a definite recommendation and instead merely suggests that some possible course of action might be effective

9. Two months ago a major shipment of pythons arrived from Africa, resulting in a great number of inexpensive pythons in pet stores. Anyone interested in buying a python, however, should beware: many pythons hatched in Africa are afflicted with a deadly liver disease. Although a few pythons recently hatched in North America have this disease, a much greater proportion of African-hatched pythons have it. The disease is difficult to detect in its early stages, and all pythons die within six months of contracting the disease.

Which one of the following statements can be properly inferred from the statements above?

(A) Some pythons hatched in North America may appear fine but will die within six months as a result of the liver disease.
(B) Pythons that hatch in Africa are more susceptible to the liver disease than are pythons that hatch in North America.
(C) Any python that has not died by the age of six months does not have the liver disease.
(D) The pythons are inexpensively priced because many of them suffer from the liver disease.
(E) Pythons hatched in neither Africa nor North America are not afflicted with the liver disease.

10. Nutritionists believe that a person's daily requirement for vitamins can readily be met by eating five servings of fruits and vegetables daily. However, most people eat far less than this. Thus, most people need to take vitamin pills.

Which one of the following statements, if true, most seriously weakens the argument?

(A) Even five servings of fruits and vegetables a day is insufficient unless the intake is varied to ensure that different vitamins are consumed.
(B) Certain commonly available fruits and vegetables contain considerably more nutrients than others.
(C) Nutritionists sometimes disagree on how much of a fruit or vegetable constitutes a complete serving.
(D) Many commonly consumed foods that are neither fruits nor vegetables are fortified by manufacturers with the vitamins found in fruits and vegetables.
(E) Fruits and vegetables are also important sources of fiber, in forms not found in vitamin pills.

11. Researcher: This fall I returned to a research site to recover the armadillos I had tagged there the previous spring. Since a large majority of the armadillos I recaptured were found within a few hundred yards of the location of their tagging last spring, I concluded that armadillos do not move rapidly into new territories.

Which one of the following is an assumption required by the researcher's argument?

(A) Of the armadillos living in the area of the tagging site last spring, few were able to avoid being tagged by the researcher.
(B) Most of the armadillos tagged the previous spring were not recaptured during the subsequent fall.
(C) Predators did not kill any of the armadillos that had been tagged the previous spring.
(D) The tags identifying the armadillos cannot be removed by the armadillos, either by accident or deliberately.
(E) A large majority of the recaptured armadillos did not move to a new territory in the intervening summer and then move back to the old territory by the fall.

GO ON TO THE NEXT PAGE.

12. Sahira: To make a living from their art, artists of great potential would have to produce work that would gain widespread popular acclaim, instead of their best work. That is why governments are justified in subsidizing artists.

Rahima: Your argument for subsidizing art depends on claiming that to gain widespread popular acclaim, artists must produce something other than their best work; but this need not be true.

In her argument, Rahima

(A) disputes an implicit assumption of Sahira's
(B) presents independent support for Sahira's argument
(C) accepts Sahira's conclusion, but for reasons different from those given by Sahira
(D) uses Sahira's premises to reach a conclusion different from that reached by Sahira
(E) argues that a standard that she claims Sahira uses is self-contradictory

13. Adult frogs are vulnerable to dehydration because of their highly permeable skins. Unlike large adult frogs, small adult frogs have such a low ratio of body weight to skin surface area that they cannot survive in arid climates. The animals' moisture requirements constitute the most important factor determining where frogs can live in the Yucatán peninsula, which has an arid climate in the north and a wet climate in the south.

The information above most strongly supports which one of the following conclusions about frogs in the Yucatán peninsula?

(A) Large adult frogs cannot coexist with small adult frogs in the wet areas.
(B) Frogs living in wet areas weigh more on average than frogs in the arid areas.
(C) Large adult frogs can live in more of the area than small adult frogs can.
(D) Fewer small adult frogs live in the south than do large adult frogs.
(E) Small adult frogs in the south have less permeable skins than small adult frogs in the north.

14. Editorial: A recent survey shows that 77 percent of people feel that crime is increasing and that 87 percent feel the judicial system should be handing out tougher sentences. Therefore, the government must firmly address the rising crime rate.

The reasoning in the editorial's argument is most vulnerable to criticism on the grounds that the argument

(A) appeals to survey results that are inconsistent because they suggest that more people are concerned about the sentencing of criminals than are concerned about crime itself
(B) presumes, without providing justification, that there is a correlation between criminal offenders being treated leniently and a high crime rate
(C) fails to consider whether other surveys showing different results have been conducted over the years
(D) fails to distinguish between the crime rate's actually rising and people's believing that the crime rate is rising
(E) presumes, without providing justification, that tougher sentences are the most effective means of alleviating the crime problem

15. Proofs relying crucially on computers provide less certainty than do proofs not requiring computers. Human cognition alone cannot verify computer-dependent proofs; such proofs can never provide the degree of certainty that attends our judgments concerning, for instance, simple arithmetical facts, which can be verified by human calculation. Of course, in these cases one often uses electronic calculators, but here the computer is a convenience rather than a supplement to human cognition.

The statements above, if true, most strongly support which one of the following?

(A) Only if a proof's result is arrived at without the help of a computer can one judge with any degree of certainty that the proof is correct.
(B) We can never be completely sure that proofs relying crucially on computers do not contain errors that humans do not detect.
(C) Whenever a computer replaces human calculation in a proof, the degree of certainty provided by the proof is reduced.
(D) If one can corroborate something by human calculation, one can be completely certain of it.
(E) It is impossible to supplement the cognitive abilities of humans by means of artificial devices such as computers.

GO ON TO THE NEXT PAGE.

16. Madden: Industrialists address problems by simplifying them, but in farming that strategy usually leads to oversimplification. For example, industrialists see water retention and drainage as different and opposite functions—that good topsoil both drains and retains water is a fact alien to industrial logic. To facilitate water retention, they use a terrace or a dam; to facilitate drainage, they use drain tile, a ditch, or a subsoiler. More farming problems are created than solved when agriculture is the domain of the industrialist, not of the farmer.

The situation as Madden describes it best illustrates which one of the following propositions?

(A) The handling of water drainage and retention is the most important part of good farming.
(B) The problems of farming should be viewed in all their complexity.
(C) Farmers are better than anyone else at solving farming problems.
(D) Industrial solutions for problems in farming should never be sought.
(E) The approach to problem solving typical of industrialists is fundamentally flawed.

17. Critic: Works of modern literature cannot be tragedies as those of ancient playwrights and storytellers were unless their protagonists are seen as possessing nobility, which endures through the calamities that befall one. In an age that no longer takes seriously the belief that human endeavors are governed by fate, it is therefore impossible for a contemporary work of literature to be a tragedy.

Which one of the following is an assumption required by the critic's argument?

(A) Whether or not a work of literature is a tragedy should not depend on characteristics of its audience.
(B) The belief that human endeavors are governed by fate is false.
(C) Most plays that were once classified as tragedies were misclassified.
(D) Those whose endeavors are not regarded as governed by fate will not be seen as possessing nobility.
(E) If an ignoble character in a work of literature endures through a series of misfortunes, that work of literature is not a tragedy.

18. Despite the efforts of a small minority of graduate students at one university to unionize, the majority of graduate students there remain unaware of the attempt. Most of those who are aware believe that a union would not represent their interests or that, if it did, it would not effectively pursue them. Thus, the graduate students at the university should not unionize, since the majority of them obviously disapprove of the attempt.

The reasoning in the argument is most vulnerable to criticism on the grounds that the argument

(A) tries to establish a conclusion simply on the premise that the conclusion agrees with a long-standing practice
(B) fails to exclude alternative explanations for why some graduate students disapprove of unionizing
(C) presumes that simply because a majority of a population is unaware of something, it must not be a good idea
(D) ignores the possibility that although a union might not effectively pursue graduate student interests, there are other reasons for unionizing
(E) blurs the distinction between active disapproval and mere lack of approval

19. Anyone who believes in democracy has a high regard for the wisdom of the masses. Griley, however, is an elitist who believes that any artwork that is popular is unlikely to be good. Thus, Griley does not believe in democracy.

The conclusion follows logically if which one of the following is assumed?

(A) Anyone who believes that an artwork is unlikely to be good if it is popular is an elitist.
(B) Anyone who believes that if an artwork is popular it is unlikely to be good does not have a high regard for the wisdom of the masses.
(C) If Griley is not an elitist, then he has a high regard for the wisdom of the masses.
(D) Anyone who does not have a high regard for the wisdom of the masses is an elitist who believes that if an artwork is popular it is unlikely to be good.
(E) Unless Griley believes in democracy, Griley does not have a high regard for the wisdom of the masses.

GO ON TO THE NEXT PAGE.

20. A recent study confirmed that salt intake tends to increase blood pressure and found that, as a result, people with high blood pressure who significantly cut their salt intake during the study had lower blood pressure by the end of the study. However, it was also found that some people who had very high salt intake both before and throughout the study maintained very low blood pressure.

Which one of the following, if true, contributes the most to an explanation of the results of the study?

(A) Study participants with high blood pressure who cut their salt intake only slightly during the study did not have significantly lower blood pressure by the end of the study.

(B) Salt intake is only one of several dietary factors associated with high blood pressure.

(C) For most people who have high blood pressure, reducing salt intake is not the most effective dietary change they can make to reduce their blood pressure.

(D) At the beginning of the study, some people who had very low salt intake also had very high blood pressure.

(E) Persons suffering from abnormally low blood pressure have heightened salt cravings, which ensure that their blood pressure does not drop too low.

21. The odds of winning any major lottery jackpot are extremely slight. However, the very few people who do win major jackpots receive a great deal of attention from the media. Thus, since most people come to have at least some awareness of events that receive extensive media coverage, it is likely that many people greatly overestimate the odds of their winning a major jackpot.

Which one of the following is an assumption on which the argument depends?

(A) Most people who overestimate the likelihood of winning a major jackpot do so at least in part because media coverage of other people who have won major jackpots downplays the odds against winning such a jackpot.

(B) Very few people other than those who win major jackpots receive a great deal of attention from the media.

(C) If it were not for media attention, most people who purchase lottery tickets would not overestimate their chances of winning a jackpot.

(D) Becoming aware of individuals who won a major jackpot leads at least some people to incorrectly estimate their own chances of winning such a jackpot.

(E) At least some people who are heavily influenced by the media do not believe that the odds of their winning a major jackpot are significant.

GO ON TO THE NEXT PAGE.

22. A book tour will be successful if it is well publicized and the author is an established writer. Julia is an established writer, and her book tour was successful. So her book tour must have been well publicized.

Which one of the following exhibits a pattern of flawed reasoning most closely parallel to the pattern of flawed reasoning exhibited by the argument above?

(A) This recipe will turn out only if one follows it exactly and uses high-quality ingredients. Arthur followed the recipe exactly and it turned out. Thus, Arthur must have used high-quality ingredients.

(B) If a computer has the fastest microprocessor and the most memory available, it will meet Aletha's needs this year. This computer met Aletha's needs last year. So it must have had the fastest microprocessor and the most memory available last year.

(C) If cacti are kept in the shade and watered more than twice weekly, they will die. This cactus was kept in the shade, and it is now dead. Therefore, it must have been watered more than twice weekly.

(D) A house will suffer from dry rot and poor drainage only if it is built near a high water table. This house suffers from dry rot and has poor drainage. Thus, it must have been built near a high water table.

(E) If one wears a suit that has double vents and narrow lapels, one will be fashionably dressed. The suit that Joseph wore to dinner last night had double vents and narrow lapels, so Joseph must have been fashionably dressed.

23. Eight large craters run in a long straight line across a geographical region. Although some of the craters contain rocks that have undergone high-pressure shocks characteristic of meteorites slamming into Earth, these shocks could also have been caused by extreme volcanic events. Because of the linearity of the craters, it is very unlikely that some of them were caused by volcanoes and others were caused by meteorites. Thus, since the craters are all different ages, they were probably caused by volcanic events rather than meteorites.

Which one of the following statements, if true, would most strengthen the argument?

(A) A similar but shorter line of craters that are all the same age is known to have been caused by volcanic activity.

(B) No known natural cause would likely account for eight meteorite craters of different ages forming a straight line.

(C) There is no independent evidence of either meteorites or volcanic activity in the region where the craters are located.

(D) There is no independent evidence of a volcanic event strong enough to have created the high-pressure shocks that are characteristic of meteorites slamming into Earth.

(E) No known single meteor shower has created exactly eight impact craters that form a straight line.

GO ON TO THE NEXT PAGE.

24. The genuine creative genius is someone who is dissatisfied with merely habitual assent to widely held beliefs; thus these rare innovators tend to anger the majority. Those who are dissatisfied with merely habitual assent to widely held beliefs tend to seek out controversy, and controversy seekers enjoy demonstrating the falsehood of popular viewpoints.

The conclusion of the argument follows logically if which one of the following is assumed?

(A) People become angry when they are dissatisfied with merely habitual assent to widely held beliefs.

(B) People who enjoy demonstrating the falsehood of popular viewpoints anger the majority.

(C) People tend to get angry with individuals who hold beliefs not held by a majority of people.

(D) People who anger the majority enjoy demonstrating the falsehood of popular viewpoints.

(E) People who anger the majority are dissatisfied with merely habitual assent to widely held beliefs.

25. Claude: When I'm having lunch with job candidates, I watch to see if they salt their food without first tasting it. If they do, I count that against them, because they're making decisions based on inadequate information.

Larissa: That's silly. It's perfectly reasonable for me to wear a sweater whenever I go into a supermarket, because I already know supermarkets are always too cool inside to suit me. And I never open a credit card offer that comes in the mail, because I already know that no matter how low its interest rate may be, it will never be worthwhile for me.

The two analogies that Larissa offers can most reasonably be interpreted as invoking which one of the following principles to criticize Claude's policy?

(A) In matters involving personal preference, performing an action without first ascertaining whether it is appropriate in the specific circumstances should not be taken as good evidence of faulty decision making, because the action may be based on a reasoned policy relating to knowledge of a general fact about the circumstances.

(B) In professional decision-making contexts, those who have the responsibility of judging other people's suitability for a job should not use observations of job-related behavior as a basis for inferring general conclusions about those people's character.

(C) General conclusions regarding a job candidate's suitability for a position should not be based exclusively on observations of the candidate's behavior in situations that are neither directly job related nor likely to be indicative of a pattern of behavior that the candidate engages in.

(D) Individuals whose behavior in specific circumstances does not conform to generally expected norms should not automatically be considered unconcerned with meeting social expectations, because such individuals may be acting in accordance with reasoned policies that they believe should be generally adopted by people in similar circumstances.

(E) Evidence that a particular individual uses bad decision-making strategies in matters of personal taste should not be considered sufficient to warrant a negative assessment of his or her suitability for a job, because any good decision maker can have occasional lapses of rationality with regard to such matters.

S T O P

IF YOU FINISH BEFORE TIME IS CALLED, YOU MAY CHECK YOUR WORK ON THIS SECTION ONLY.
DO NOT WORK ON ANY OTHER SECTION IN THE TEST.

Acknowledgment is made to the following sources from which material has been adapted for use in this test booklet:

Elizabeth Wayland Barber, *Women's Work: The First 20,000 Years: Women, Cloth, and Society in Early Times.* ©1994 by
  Elizabeth Wayland Barber.

Wait for the supervisor's instructions before you open the page to the topic.
Please print and sign your name and write the date in the designated spaces below.
Time: 35 Minutes

General Directions

You will have 35 minutes in which to plan and write an essay on the topic inside. Read the topic and the accompanying directions carefully. You will probably find it best to spend a few minutes considering the topic and organizing your thoughts before you begin writing. In your essay, be sure to develop your ideas fully, leaving time, if possible, to review what you have written. **Do not write on a topic other than the one specified. Writing on a topic of your own choice is not acceptable.**

No special knowledge is required or expected for this writing exercise. Law schools are interested in the reasoning, clarity, organization, language usage, and writing mechanics displayed in your essay. How well you write is more important than how much you write.

Confine your essay to the blocked, lined area on the front and back of the separate Writing Sample Response Sheet. Only that area will be reproduced for law schools. Be sure that your writing is legible.

Both this topic sheet and your response sheet must be turned over to the testing staff before you leave the room.

LSAC ®

Topic Code		Print Your Full Name Here		
087205	Last	First		M.I.

Date		Sign Your Name Here
/ /		

Scratch Paper
Do not write your essay in this space.

LSAT® Writing Sample Topic

Directions: The scenario presented below describes two choices, either one of which can be supported on the basis of the information given. Your essay should consider both choices and argue for one over the other, based on the two specified criteria and the facts provided. There is no "right" or "wrong" choice: a reasonable argument can be made for either.

A local amateur astronomical association is going to build a new observatory that will house a medium-sized telescope near the association's home town of Brenton. The association has narrowed the possible building sites down to two. Using the facts below, write an essay in which you argue for one site over the other based on the following two criteria:

- The site should provide seeing conditions for the use of the telescope that minimize atmospheric haze and sources of light pollution.
- The site should facilitate holding public observing sessions and lectures on astronomy for people from Brenton.

The first site is on top of a 2,000 foot (600 meter) ridge within a small forest park. This height is above some of the atmosphere's haze. To reach the summit, visitors must drive up a gravel road that is narrow and winding. Light pollution from a relatively distant megalopolis seriously affects about a quarter of the night sky. Currently, the land surrounding the park is mostly undeveloped farmland. How much will be developed is unpredictable.

The second site is almost at sea level in the middle of a large forest park. Some of the land near the site is swampy. City lights cause some light pollution across about a quarter of the night sky. The roads from Brenton to the site are all paved and in good condition. The travel time to this site from Brenton is about a third less than that to the first site. Unscheduled visitors are more likely at this site than at the first site. They could disturb the work of the amateur astronomers.

WP-Q087

Scratch Paper
Do not write your essay in this space.

Directions:

1. Use the Answer Key on the next page to check your answers.

2. Use the Scoring Worksheet below to compute your raw score.

3. Use the Score Conversion Chart to convert your raw score into the 120-180 scale.

Scoring Worksheet

1. Enter the number of questions you answered correctly in each section.

	Number Correct
SECTION I.	_____
SECTION II	_____
SECTION III.	_____
SECTION IV.	_____

2. Enter the sum here: _____
   This is your Raw Score.

Conversion Chart
For Converting Raw Score to the 120-180 LSAT Scaled Score
LSAT Form 9LSN81

Reported Score	Raw Score Lowest	Raw Score Highest
180	99	101
179	—*	—*
178	98	98
177	97	97
176	96	96
175	95	95
174	—*	—*
173	94	94
172	93	93
171	91	92
170	90	90
169	89	89
168	88	88
167	86	87
166	85	85
165	84	84
164	82	83
163	80	81
162	79	79
161	77	78
160	75	76
159	74	74
158	72	73
157	70	71
156	69	69
155	67	68
154	65	66
153	63	64
152	61	62
151	60	60
150	58	59
149	56	57
148	54	55
147	53	53
146	51	52
145	49	50
144	47	48
143	46	46
142	44	45
141	42	43
140	41	41
139	39	40
138	38	38
137	36	37
136	34	35
135	33	33
134	31	32
133	30	30
132	29	29
131	27	28
130	26	26
129	25	25
128	23	24
127	22	22
126	21	21
125	20	20
124	18	19
123	17	17
122	16	16
121	15	15
120	0	14

*There is no raw score that will produce this scaled score for this form.

SECTION I

1.	C	8.	E	15.	D	22.	C
2.	D	9.	E	16.	E	23.	C
3.	E	10.	B	17.	B	24.	E
4.	E	11.	A	18.	C	25.	A
5.	A	12.	D	19.	D	26.	A
6.	A	13.	B	20.	E		
7.	B	14.	D	21.	C		

SECTION II

1.	B	8.	D	15.	A	22.	C
2.	E	9.	C	16.	B	23.	B
3.	E	10.	A	17.	A	24.	A
4.	D	11.	B	18.	E	25.	C
5.	C	12.	A	19.	C	26.	B
6.	E	13.	E	20.	D	27.	D
7.	A	14.	B	21.	E		

SECTION III

1.	E	8.	B	15.	B	22.	B
2.	C	9.	C	16.	B	23.	B
3.	E	10.	B	17.	C		
4.	A	11.	A	18.	C		
5.	E	12.	B	19.	D		
6.	C	13.	D	20.	B		
7.	C	14.	D	21.	E		

SECTION IV

1.	E	8.	B	15.	B	22.	C
2.	C	9.	A	16.	B	23.	B
3.	A	10.	D	17.	D	24.	B
4.	C	11.	E	18.	E	25.	A
5.	A	12.	A	19.	B		
6.	D	13.	C	20.	E		
7.	A	14.	D	21.	D		

LSAT® Prep Tools

LSAT ItemWise®

Get to know the LSAT

LSAC's popular, online LSAT familiarization tool, *LSAT ItemWise*:

- includes all three types of LSAT questions—logical reasoning, analytical reasoning, and reading comprehension;

- keeps track of your answers; and

- shows you explanations as to why answers are correct or incorrect.

Although it is best to use our paper-and-pencil *Official LSAT PrepTest®* products to fully prepare for the LSAT, you can enhance your preparation by understanding all three question types and why your answers are right or wrong.

ItemWise includes an introduction to the new reading comprehension question type—comparative reading—with sample questions and explanations.

LSAC account holders get unlimited online access to *ItemWise* for the length of the account.

$18